SOCIAL MEDIA
MARKETING TRICKS
2020

Tips and Advice for How to Reach One Million Followers through Instagram, YouTube, Facebook and Twitter: From beginner to professional

Jason Miller - Ray Robbins

TABLE OF CONTENTS

INTRODUCTIONS 6

CHAPTER-ONE:

SOCIAL MEDIA OR SOCIAL NETWORKS 8

SOCIAL MEDIA TRACKING 9

SOCIAL NETWORK METRICS 10

STRATEGIES FOR SOCIAL MEDIA MARKETING 13

IDENTIFYING WINNING STRATEGIES FOR MARKETING ON SOCIAL MEDIA... 20

CHAPTER-TWO:

FACEBOOK MARKETING 2020... 42

TIPS FOR SUCCESSFUL MARKETING STRATEGY ON FACEBOOK 61

HERE'S HOW TO CREATE A POWERFUL FACEBOOK PAGE 66

OPTIMIZE POSTS ON YOUR FACEBOOK PAGE................ 69

FACEBOOK MARKETING: GUIDE TO GET CUSTOMERS AND SALES WITH A SMALL BUSINESS............................. 75

HOW TO MAKE MONEY ON FACEBOOK PAGE 84

CHAPTER-THREE:

INSTAGRAM MARKETING 2020 88

HOW TO CUSTOMIZE YOUR INSTAGRAM? 93

TIPS TO GETTING FOLLOWERS ON INSTAGRAM 105

HOW TO CREATE AN INSTAGRAM MARKETING STRATEGY FOR YOUR BUSINESS 111

HOW TO OPTIMIZE ACCOUNT AND SELL 119

HOW DOES THE INSTAGRAM ALGORITHM WORK 122

HOW TO BEAT THE INSTAGRAM ALGORITHM 124

MONETIZING YOUR INSTAGRAM PAGE 130

CHAPTER-FOUR:

YOUTUBE MARKETING 2020 139

STEPS TO CREATE YOUR YOUTUBE CHANNEL 153

STEPS TO MONETIZE YOUTUBE VIDEOS 160

TRICKS TO IMPROVE YOUR YOUTUBE CHANNEL 163

CHAPTER-FIVE:

TWITTER MARKETING 2020 175

HOW TO LEVERAGE TWITTER AS A MARKETING TOOL 178

MARKETING ON TWITTER IN 2020 180

COMMON MISTAKES THAT ARE MADE ON TWITTER 183

HOW TO CREATE YOUR LIST ON TWITTER 187

TWITTER ANALYTICS 189

HOW TO EARN MONEY USING TWITTER 197

CONCLUSION 202

INTRODUCTIONS

Facebook, Twitter, Instagram and YouTube; names that come to mind when we talk about social networks (RRSS). Those are the 4 best known, but today there are so many that it is impossible to find a complete list.

They are part of our day to day, and an increasingly important part, so it is convenient to know them. To know what a social network is we can go to a dictionary.

Social network is defined as a service of the information society that offers users a communication platform through the Internet so that they generate a profile with their personal data, facilitating the creation of communities based on criteria common and allowing the communication of its users so that they can interact through messages, share information, images or videos, allowing these publications to be immediately accessible by all users in your group.

A very complete definition but a little dense, so we go with a more affordable definition and of walking around the house:

A social network is a digital space in which users interact, communicating with each other or sharing information.

Thanks to social networks, users form communities

based on common interests, friendship relationships or professional relationships. Depending on the user's objectives (which can be a real person or a brand), social networks can be categorized into:

Generic social networks, which aim to socialize through the Internet, Professional social networks, which work to connect colleagues or to look for work.

Thematic social networks, which are reduced to a specific topic (there are social networks for lovers of cinema, photography, fashion).

CHAPTER ONE

SOCIAL MEDIA OR SOCIAL NETWORKS

You probably already got confused between networks and social media. But it is important to clarify that they are not the same thing. Therefore, we are going to differentiate them right now.

As I told you, social networks are the groups of connections and relationships we have with other people. And social media are platforms that guarantee that happens.

Still confused? It is clear when we understand that both can serve as platforms to maintain our networks of relationships, however, social networks have that as their main feature and are within what we classify as social media.

While social media are platforms that have as their main function, the mass exchange of content and transmission of information, such as blogs, pages and even YouTube itself.

Summing up all that, we can affirm that social networks are a category within social media. Places where we can interact with people we know, but in which at all times we are exposed to an immensity of content.

SOCIAL MEDIA TRACKING

Your work does not end when you press the submit button. The truth is this is just the beginning. You need to be aware of everything that happens in your social networks and that is why I will talk about what you need to be aware of and good practices:

Comments

They are very important for your strategy and show who is willing to interact with your brand. Therefore, if someone cared enough to comment something, like or react to that comment and respond when necessary. The famous use of gifs is approved, but always with moderation and consistency.

A mention can be very good, as well as sharing a content or praise, but it can also be a bad thing, like someone expressing dissatisfaction with your company. Stay tuned for this! In the end, this person shared the content and that can be propagated. Respond with sincerity and solve the situation.

Evaluations

You probably saw the evaluation of a page on Facebook. And despite being present only in this network, evaluations deserve your attention. In the end, they serve as a thermometer of how people are considering your brand and are public.

Occasionally something negative may arise, but one of the main virtues of any social media professional is to remain calm and resolve that situation efficiently.

It shows sensitivity and guarantees that this problem will be solved. People want to feel empowered and heard. Remember it!

Chat

Currently the chats in social networks, whatever they are, function as the SAC 2.0 model in social networks. And that is where most of the time a consumer will solve their doubts, seek help, solve some question or express some dissatisfaction.

This is perhaps one of the most important spaces of social networks, it is a personal contact you have with a certain user, and the impression you leave represents the image of your brand for him.

SOCIAL NETWORK METRICS

If you came here without understanding the importance of data and analysis of results for a social media strategy, I failed my mission. But I will solve this by showing you now what metrics you need to accompany to ensure your success. Join me a little more:

Scope

The scope is what will show how many users your post

reached. This does not mean that they interacted with the publication or stopped reading it.

So why is this important to you? Because it will help you understand how your posts are performing according to the Facebook algorithm.

Based on this analysis you will be able to adapt your strategy and optimize what is necessary for your publications to reach your audience.

Traffic

If your social networks are not bringing traffic to your website or blog in any way, you are doing something very wrong. Understanding how you take a user through the funnel of your company is essential and social networks have a very important role: the acquisition.

Interest

It is here that you see who are the true followers of your brand and who is willing to interact with you. But what does interest really mean? It is the number of likes, shares and comments that your posts have.

It is going to show you mainly how relevant and attractive your strategy has been, in addition to helping you interact with your audience.

Channel growth

The larger your fan base, the more people you have the chance to reach. But, this can be a treacherous number, because not always the growth of your channel will mean a growth of interest or scope. It is important you put more effort as that is what will make it possible.

Vanity Metrics

When talking about treacherous, we need to talk about vanity metrics. Do you know what they are? Basically, they are numbers that will surely leave you happy, you should not feel guilty about it but they do not bring real results for your company.

Did your post have 5000 likes? Congratulations, you probably deserved it. But that will not help you make any decisions and does not provide insights about future actions. Then you can accompany them, just don't spend so much time with them.

If you got here Congratulations! We hope you can take advantage of everything learned to take your social media strategy to another level and multiply your results.

But as we well know, it is never enough and surely you can still discover more about this incredible world of social networks. To always take this knowledge wherever you go and consult it when you need, I recommend you download our checklist so you don't miss anything on your social media profile.

STRATEGIES FOR SOCIAL MEDIA MARKETING

There are many possibilities in social media marketing. The individual social networks offer different forms to be present in the network. But behind all these uses is a common social media strategy. Before you go You should ask yourself the following questions about your company and social network products:

- Situation analysis?

- What does the target group look like?

- What are the goals you want to achieve?

- Which channel is suitable for this?

- Which resources are there?

- How can I perform a success check?

Situation analysis

The first is the question of which social network you are already using. Are these enough or do I need to revise them? How does your competition work on social media? If the use of social media marketing is already common in the industry, you need to work harder to implement the strategy. You also need to know the time and money you can spend pursuing social media strategies.

Target group

The important point is the target audience. If you know who is most likely to use your product or service, you need to know where this viewer is on the social media platform. If you know who you want to deal with, you can get clear images of individual content forms.

Goal definition

Clearly defined goals facilitate the implementation of each strategy. Your main goal may be to sell your product, but it should not be the focus of a social media strategy. This overflows with each user's time. However, one goal is to build a brand, acquire new customers, build efficient customer service, or communicate with customers as fans.

Channel selection

When choosing the right social media channel, you must head towards the target group. For example, if your audience is primarily focused on video content and images, you will need to adjust the content accordingly. You can also create videos about the product and provide informational videos. For example, the YouTube platform is perfect for this.

Resource

This includes both time and financial budgets. After all, working on social media requires almost daily employment. You need to post regularly or respond to user requests. You 'll also need to clarify in advance how much you 'll invest in banner ads and content boost. A professional social media manager should help as soon as you need two or three social media networks.

Success control

Each marketing metric also requires a review of success. ROI is used for social media marketing, which is also part of online marketing. This return on investment shows the amount of profit generated by social media marketing measures is compared to their cost.

Examples of social media strategies

Social media campaigns are most successful when they spread automatically. Postings that go viral are the best solution for social media marketing. Whether content becomes viral or not can not be predicted. There is no panacea, but there are some strategies that offer the highest chances to make a campaign viral.

The online marketing mix

Online Marketing pursues the goals of increasing the visibility of its own company and increasing the number of visitors on the Internet. This happens with the right marketing mix. The following components are available for this:

Website or Conversion Rate Optimization (CRO)

SEM and SEO (Search Engine Marketing or Optimization)

Content Marketing

Social Media Marketing

E-mail marketing

Affiliate Marketing

Viral Campaign Marketing

Online PR

Website - or conversion rate optimization (CRO)

The website tracks multiple destinations simultaneously. It is primarily there to generate sales but also to increase the commitment of users. This means that users can order your products on your website and they can search through your assortment. You can also offer interesting downloads on your website and introduce your company in detail. With Conversion Rate Optimization you can improve your website in terms of the user journey and simplify the actions of the users you want on your site.

SEM

This abbreviation stands for Search Engine Marketing. This method includes SEA (Search Engine

Advertisement) and SEO (Search Engine Optimization). Especially keywords play a crucial role. But also internal links within your website, technical aspects as well as link building (generating backlinks) are part of it.

Content Marketing

Content Marketing deals with the content that can be found on your website. This can be texts or pictures, but also videos or livestreams. In any case, this content should offer added value for the user as well as being interesting and up-to-date. Not for nothing is mentioned always and everywhere: Content is King. If your content is not worth reading and offers no added value, users will lose in large quantities.

Social Media Marketing

Social media marketing deals with the dissemination of corporate content on the pages of social networks. So it's also part of online marketing.

E-mail marketing

E-mail marketing sends e-mails or newsletters at regular intervals. While e-mail marketing was the undisputed number one in direct contact with customers a few years ago, the marketing channel is now facing competition from messenger marketing via Facebook Messenger, What's App and Co., which is also made possible by social media

Affiliate Marketing

This is understood as an online marketing system operated by commercial providers. This provider remunerates its distribution partners with commissions. The provider provides advertising material that the affiliate marketer can use. If this use leads to purchase agreements, the marketer receives a commission.

Viral campaign marketing

Viral marketing primarily uses the social network to spread advertising messages. One of the hallmarks of marketing that becomes viral is the rapid spread on the Internet. An interesting and usually strange message is clicked in a kind of chain reaction and made viral. The term comes from medicine, when viruses as pathogens have a rapid spread.

Online PR

Online PR is a form of modern public relations. Content is not communicated via traditional channels such as TV or radio, but over the Internet. Online PR specializes in a social network such as Twitter.

To look for a suitable social network, it is advisable to look at the statistics. The Hamburg-based communications consultancy Faktenkontor, for example, together with the market research institute Toluna, has recently examined the usage habits of Germans. Advertising on social networks is as good as advertising on TV. Above all, Facebook advertising dominates. About a quarter of all Germans felt led by Facebook advertising to buy a product. Around 20% of YouTube users purchased a product or used a service as a result of advertising. The platform as a social network thus lies in the advertising hyperspace between print media and the radio.

Age-specific, there are also differences in the frequency of use of individual social networks. Snapchat and Instagram are very popular with young people in particular. Around 71% of all users between the ages of 14 and 19 use these networks. But also Pinterest is in high demand among the young people. More than a third use this platform as a social network.

For the older users, ages 30 and up, Xing and LinkedIn are at the top of the list.

How much does Social Media Marketing cost ?

The cost of social media marketing depends primarily on the needs of your business. A lump sum, which must be spent for it, there is just as little as in conventional advertising. However, all social media-related activities require staffing. Websites must be maintained and user requests must be responded to. This requires constant attention to the topic as well as a permanent presence in the social media. This personnel expenditure costs above all time and money.

Certainly, viral marketing is the cheapest. Videos that become viral are self-tracking. But that does not happen without previous planning and good content.

Companies that already have a PR department recruiting their own staff. Others set up their own department. A third option is to hire an external marketing agency.

If you now calculate all the resulting costs, you can expect that a social media campaign will require at least a budget of 10,000 euros. The individual possibilities you see here again briefly summarized.

Recruitment of own staff

Establishment of a separate department

Commissioning of an external agency

IDENTIFYING WINNING STRATEGIES FOR MARKETING ON SOCIAL MEDIA

Here's how to design your social networking strategy in steps:

- Identify your goals
- Identify your target audiences
- Select the right platforms
- Master the algorithms
- Adopt the right content strategy
- Monitor and improve your performance

1. Identify your goals

Social media is a channel of promotion and not an end in itself. The social networking strategy is part of a much broader context: your web marketing strategy. In order to be effective, your strategic social media plan must be aligned with the growth objectives of your SME in the long and short term.

That's why the first step in any social media strategy is to determine what you hope to gain from your efforts.

What are your strategic goals

Do you want to share your business with people who have never heard of it? Or inspire your current customers to do business with you again?

When it comes to web marketing, your prospective customers can be captured at different stages of their buying process:

- Awareness / Exploration
- Interest / Consideration
- Conversion
- Loyalty

So, your strategic goals will largely depend on the stage at which you want to reach your prospects:

HOW TO USE SOCIAL MEDIA TO ACHIEVE THESE GOALS

No matter which stage of the sales process you want to target, you will be able to use your social media strategy to achieve your goals:

Build your brand awareness: Social media advertising allows you to target the individuals most likely to be interested in your business to showcase your brand.

Convince your prospects: the strategic use of hash tags on social media and the optimization of your video referencing on you tube allow you to capture your prospects when they are actively looking for your products and services.

Generate sales: Integrating a Facebook store or Instagram Shopping allows you to convert your subscribers into customers without having to leave the platform.

Build customer loyalty: With social media, you can continue to interact with your customers after their purchase and even target them with remarketing campaigns on Facebook Ads.

In short: once you have defined your goals, you will be able to identify the actions to take to achieve them and maximize your efforts.

What are your performance indicators

An objective will never be attainable if it is not quantifiable or measurable. KPIs examples you can define in your social media strategy to guide its execution:

Performance indicators for your organic efforts:

- Size of your community
- Scope of your publications
- Commitment
- clicks
- Messages / Calls

Performance indicators for your paid advertising:

- Click through rate
- Conversion rate
- Cost per commitment (mentions "I like", comments, reactions, sharing ...)
- Cost per click
- Cost per call

2. Identify your target audiences

Does your company sell to individuals (B2C) or businesses (B2B)? Are your products or services designed for individuals residing in a specific geographic area?

To answer these questions and more, while still keeping your target audience in mind, we strongly suggest you define a persona in your social media strategy.

What is a persona

This is your typical client profile and its demographic, psychological and behavioral characteristics. When drawing the portrait of your persona, you can include:

- His age
- His sex
- His job
- Where he / she lives
- His interests
- His lifestyle
- Her personality

This type of description gives you a much clearer idea of the needs and expectations of your prospective customers. This makes it easier for you to adapt your editorial tone to your community and create more engaging content to reach your goals quickly.

3. Select the right platforms

Now that your persona is identified, you need to determine the best way to reach them. What social media platforms do they use?

You would not use Instagram, a photo sharing platform, to sell to the blind, or Snapchat to sell to the elderly. In short: make sure you target your potential customers where they are.

Here are some general information to help you choose your platform, among the 7 most popular social networks:

WHO USES FACEBOOK?

- Number of users: 2 billion
- Suitable for B2B and B2C
- Demographic characteristics:
- 56% men / 44% women
- 65% of users are over 35
- Popular in urban and rural environments

WHO USES YOUTUBE?

- Number of users: 1.5 billion
- Suitable for B2B and B2C
- Demographic characteristics:
- 62% of users are men
- 61% are between 16-34 years old

WHO USES INSTAGRAM?

- Number of users: 800 million
- More suitable for B2C
- Demographic characteristics:
- Most popular with women: 38% of women use Instagram, compared to 26% of men.
- Popular among 15-30 years old
- Much more popular with users living in urban areas

WHO USES TWITTER?

- Number of users: 350 million
- Suitable for B2C and B2B
- Demographic characteristics:
- 50-50 Men / Women
- Strong press and influencers / bloggers

WHO USES SNAPCHAT?

- Number of users: 180 million
- Much better suited to B2C
- Demographic characteristics:
- 70% of users are women
- 70% of users are under 34

WHO USES LINKEDIN?

- Number of users: 106 million
- Much more suitable for B2B
- Demographic characteristics:
- 31% of men and 27% of women use Linkedin
- Strong use of people with high incomes

WHO USES PINTEREST?

- Number of users: 100 million
- Suitable for B2C and B2B
- Demographic characteristics:
- 70% of users are women

You can also use this grid to quickly determine which

platforms you should focus on in your social media strategy based on your business profile:

4. Master the algorithms

Once your platforms have been identified and your social networking pages created and optimized

Before you start production, optimization and dissemination of your content, you must first master your platforms ... and more precisely: their algorithms.

These are mathematical formulas used each time a publication is created to determine whether it deserves to be featured on the users' news feed.

As you will have understood, mastering how these algorithms work is a decisive factor in your ability to have good results. Although the algorithms are not all the same, their logic is very similar.

Here are, for example, the criteria on which Edge Rank, the facebook algorithm, is based to disseminate your organic publications:

Affinity: the propensity of users to engage with the content of your page in the past

Performance: the number of likes, reactions, comments, sharing of the publication

The type of content: text, image, video

5. Adopt the right content strategy

Once the algorithm is well understood, you are ready to feed your pages strategically. To do this, you will have to work on three levels: the creation of quality content, the strategic and effective dissemination of this content, and finally the optimization of the conversations it generates.

Here's how to optimize your social media at each of these steps:

- Create quality content
- Talk about what interests your persona
- Generate conversations
- Bet on a superior graphic quality
- Adapt your content to each platform
- Use engaging formats
- Put yourself in ephemeral content
- Enjoy user-generated content
- Adopt good dissemination practices
- Plan your publications
- Publish at the right time
- Use advertising
- Optimize your publications for conversion
- Use influencers
- Encourage making contact

5 Create quality content

Talk about what interests your persona

Nobody wants to go to a dinner party with friends and sit next to someone who only talks about himself ... It's the same on social media.

While the goal of a social media strategy is obviously to use your social networks to promote your business and talk about your products, put yourself in your persona's shoes instead.

What would you like to see on the Company pages that you follow? What type of content would you react to? What kind of publications would you share with your friends? What would challenge you?

To answer all these questions, there is nothing better than including a social media watch in your social networking strategy.

You can also vary your content by applying these tips:

- Promote entertaining, useful or inspiring publications
- Tell stories
- Reveal your imperfections and humanize your business
- Do not be too commercial
- Get out of your comfort zone and introduce new topics from time to time, or try new formats of publications.

B. Generate conversations

Humanize your brand on social media by generating conversations with - and between - your customers.

To do this, offer useful, entertaining or inspiring content that your subscribers will be able to share and want to share. You can also ask questions or ask your subscribers' opinions to stimulate debate or encourage them to share their opinions.

Be sure to respond to comments that your fans take the trouble to leave you: the prospect of getting an answer encourages them to comment again and encourages other subscribers to do the same.

C. Bet on superior graphic quality

The graphic quality of your social media reflects your professionalism and credibility ... Do not take it lightly!

From strategic thinking to execution, you will need to focus on the quality of your publications at every stage of your social media strategy. To ensure you provide satisfying content, here are some good practices to follow:

Make sure to re-read your texts: are they persona oriented? Are they useful for your fans? Do they contain errors? Check the quality of the visual or video content: does it represent your brand? Is it rich and well done? Is it adapted to the social media platform used?

Follow the best practices of each platform: emojis,

hashtags, targeting, hours of publication etc. In order to be well armed for the production of quality content on your social networks, we recommend the following tools:

By applying these tips and using the right tools, we are confident that you will stand out from your competition and get the attention of users!

D. Adapt your content to each platform

Although many productivity apps and tools allow you to link your social networking accounts to automatically post the same content to one and the other, we recommend that you avoid these types of solutions.

These social media platforms are all used differently and involve its own content, tailored to its users: You can adapt and atomize your content for reuse on other platforms, as long as you respect the editorial tone of each for maximum success.

E. Use engaging formats

Here's a recent analysis of the Buzzsumo site , made on more than 68 million publications, video content is the format generating the most commitment, followed by images.

Here is the preferred format according to the chosen platform:

Facebook:

- Image or Photo 360
- Video or Lives
- Carousel
- Questions (with GIFs or images)
- Stories

Youtube :

- Videos
- Instagram:
- Photo
- Videos on IGTV (less than 10 minutes)
- Insta Stories

Twitter:

- Short texts
- Pictures
- Videos
- Retweet & mentions

Snapchat:

- Stories

Linkedin:

- Photo

- Article sharing
- infographics

Pinterest:

- pins

F. Put yourself in ephemeral content

Ephemeral content is all content on social media programmed to disappear after 24 hours. More specifically, these are stories, introduced by Snapchat and recently popularized more by Instagram, before being taken up again by Facebook.

The main objection to marketers when it comes to ephemeral content is that, in theory, their production may seem like a waste of time. Why take the time to create content that is inherently doomed to disappear after a day?

In fact, it is precisely this urgent aspect that intrigues Internet users and pushes them to look at your stories and to make the suggestions that you offer them.

With the recent integration of Instagram Shopping Stories, this publication format is all the more interesting since it facilitates the access of your subscribers to your catalog of products online.

Use the Stories format to talk about the scenes of your business or your employees, to offer temporary offers and to generate a sense of scarcity and urgency among your subscribers.

G. Take advantage of user-generated content to fuel your social networking strategy

You are not alone in being able to feed your social media content: Internet users can also contribute to fill your pages with publications.

Unlike the content you create, the intention of which is clearly to promote your business, the User Generated Content (or UGC) is created and distributed by the customer (or user), of his own free will.

It can be:

- comments
- Customers' opinion
- Publications on a forum
- Podcasts / Videos
- Pictures
- Blog articles
- Tweets, Facebook posts, etc.

The Facebook contest or Instagram are a particularly effective way to encourage your users to create content for indirectly promoting your brand. This content allows you to access the social circle of your subscribers and put your products forward to find new prospects.

For example, Apple's #shotoniphone campaign, which encouraged people to share photos taken on their iPhones on Instagram, has more than 5 million participants:

USER-GENERATED CONTENT

Such campaigns are very engaging and give you access to a large pool of content that you can reuse in your publications (crediting the source, of course!). Do not hesitate to use it to complement your social networking strategy!

2. Adopt good dissemination practices

A. Plan your publications

Scheduling your publications early and scheduling them for automatic publication can save you a lot of time and make your efforts more effective.

So you can better optimize your Facebook and other publications, align your content with different holidays and important events, and always respect the good publication frequencies:

- Facebook: 1 to 2 times a day
- Youtube: 1 to 2 times a week
- Instagram: 3 to 4 times a week
- Twitter: 3 to 5 times a day
- Snapchat: 7 times a week
- Linkedin: 2 to 3 times a week

- Pinterest: Several times a day
- Hootsuite and Buffer are the popular management platforms that allow you to schedule your publications in advance.

A similar Instagram tool is Later , which also allows you to save hashtags groups and automatically add them to your posts:

Instagram tools for publishing time slots

B. Publish at the right time

The type of content you share and your frequency of publication are not the only factors influenced by your choice of platform ... You will also need to adjust the moments you publish in your social media strategy:

When to publish on Facebook:

From 12h to 15h on Monday, Wednesday, Thursday, and Friday

Between noon and 1 pm on Saturday and Sunday

When to publish on Twitter - B2B:

From 12h to 15h from Monday to Friday, the peak arriving at 15h

When to post on Twitter - B2C:

Before 9am Monday to Friday

At noon and 5 pm Monday to Friday

When to publish on Linkedin:

7:45 am Monday to Thursday

10:45 Monday to Thursday

12:45 pm Monday to Thursday

5:45 pm Monday to Thursday

When to publish on Instagram:

From Tuesday to Friday

Between 11h and 13h

Between 17h and 20h

Of course, these slots reflect averages, but do not apply to all companies in the same way. It is suggested you identify the best social media publishing moments for your industry and target audience to enrich your social media strategy.

For detailed explanations of the procedure, see our article " When to publish on your social media in 2018 ".

C. Use advertising in your social media strategy

Social media ads will be particularly useful to help you discover your products and services to your target audience or to build loyalty among your existing customers.

If you want to include advertising in your social media strategy, our Facebook advertising guides and Instagram advertising will help you optimize your ads to reach your goals faster.

3. Optimize your social media strategy for conversion

A. Use influencers

If you have a very strong social networking strategy, then it is good, you need a little help once in a while to build trust with your prospects. Influencers are individuals who have achieved a certain level of awareness on social media that are willing to promote businesses to their community.

Today, 75% of Internet users report having already purchased a product following the recommendations of an influencer . And yes! Since it's not about brands but about well-known personalities, influencers are more confident about consumers, especially if they express their opinion about a product or service:

That's why influencer marketing is so useful: it's about building on the reputation of one of these celebrities to make your promotions and boost your conversions. To take advantage of this popularity, you will need to identify the influencers whose community most resembles your persona, get in touch with them through emails or personalized direct messages and negotiate the terms of your collaboration.

Does all this seem intimidating? Do not worry; we've designed, just for you, a comprehensive guide to influencer marketing to help you in this step of your social media strategy.

B. Encourage making contact

Your prospect has discovered you through user-generated content, ads or influencers, and appreciates your quality publications ... What's next?

The next step in your social media strategy: turn your subscribers into customers by encouraging them to get in touch with you on your pages!

To do this, you have several options:

Add calls to action in your publications (call us, write to us ...)

Add a "contact us" button in your Facebook ads

Create chatbots to automatically answer your customers etc.

It is advised you to start by activating messenger on your Facebook page so that your customers can easily join you in private. Here's how to proceed:

Access the settings of your Facebook page

In the left column, click Settings

Scroll down and in the Messages section, click Edit

Select the option "Allow visitors to my Page to contact me privately by displaying the Message button"

Click Save Changes

6. Monitor and improve your performance

If you've taken the time to set your goals, it's good to make sure you reach them! What impact did your efforts have on your visibility, your reputation, your sales.

To find out, pick up your performance indicators and measure them once your social media strategy is deployed:

To analyze your social media profile, use Facebook Insights, Instagram Insights, or Twitter Analytics and determine:

The size of your community

Your organic reach

Your level of commitment

mentions "I like"

comments

shares / retweets

etc.

facebook statistics

To analyze the performance of your Facebook and Instagram ads, use the Facebook Ads Manager and watch for:

Your cost per action (CPA)

Your paid reach

Provided you are interested in the effect of social networking strategy on your traffic and conversions, use Google Analytics and measure:

The volume of social traffic received by your site

The bounce rate of this social traffic

Average time spent on your site by your social traffic

The number of leads collected from social traffic

Take the time to compare your results before and after the start of your social networking strategy and monitor its evolution so that you can adjust your efforts as you go along and maximize your performance.

CHAPTER TWO

FACEBOOK MARKETING 2020

Facebook is the main social network that exists in the world, a network of virtual links, whose main objective is to provide support to produce and share content. It came to expand the possibilities of social relationship and caused a sensitive revolution in the world of communications.

Marketing was no stranger to this change finding in this modality a fertile ground for new concepts and approaches. Facebook is the social network that more users have in the world. There are about 2.2 million users and in it you can find familiar people, participate in interest groups, share content, send and receive messages, make contacts, search, advertise, etc.

Among social networks, it is the one that users choose most often. Facebook is currently the most accessed website in the world. Thanks to its success and great adherence, it is considered as the network that directly influences the politics, culture and public opinion of the users.

But how did that phenomenon begin? What was the trajectory of the founders until today? What are the main resources of this website?

What is Facebook

Facebook is the largest of the social networks : it has 2 billion active users worldwide and turned 14 years old on February 4, 2018. Through this network, you can find familiar people, interact with them, participate in Groups that discuss topics of your interest, share content (images, text, video), send and receive messages, make contacts, search, make announcements, etc.

Therefore, being on Facebook, understanding its operation and the resources it offers is a fundamental step for those who want to expand their business or become known, expand their reach and their digital marketing strategies .

In it, it is possible to create a personal profile or a Fanpage , and interact with other people connected to the site, through the exchange of instant messages, the sharing of content and the famous "likes" in user posts.

In addition to performing these functions, it also allows you to participate in groups according to the interests of people and needs within the social network.

As of today this is the best known forms of connection and is also used to perform quick information searches; In addition to working as a kind of contact centralizer.

CTA marketing on Facebook

HISTORY

The history of the most used social network in the world began in 2003, under the name of Facemash, inside a room at Harvard University.

The site was created by students Mark Zuckerberg, Chris Hughes, Dustin Moskovitz and Brazilian Eduardo Saverin, who were in the second year of the university. With Facemash, it was possible to choose, which were the most attractive girls on campus, from comparison of photos that were collected from the University's security system

It is clear that these types of websites soon aroused the fury of Harvard students and executives, who quickly closed it. At the time, Mark suffered a series of accusations as a violation of privacy and security, facing serious problems at the university.

A short time later, the student began programming the code of a new virtual network with the name of "the facebook", which would later be used, too, by students from other nearby universities.

On this site, it was possible to create virtual friendship ties between university students. And finally, Facebook

The expansion continued, and in the summer of 2005, Facebook was officially opened with its original name, shortly after Mark Zuckerberg's advisor Sean Parker, co-founder of Nepster, suggested the subtle move of the name.

As of 2006, access was released for high school students and also for company workers in general and they were no longer just university students who could benefit from the use of the network.

Soon after, anyone over the age of 13 could connect to Facebook, providing simple information such as name, surname, email, date of birth and gender.

In 2011, the site became the largest photo server in the world. Already at the end of the same year, the number of users who entered Facebook on the cell phone exceeded 350 million.

Today that number is more than double, as well as its unquestionable success and users registered on the network, became 2 billion. Many people stopped using Facebook just as a way to connect with friends and went on to see it as a work tool, as well as a means of disseminating companies and brands.

Social network, the movie

The film that tells the story behind Facebook was critically acclaimed as the best of 2010, receiving several awards, in addition to the Oscar as best adapted screenplay, best edition and best soundtrack.

In it, the trajectory of Mark Zuckerberg is shown, and

also the complications that he had to go through since the creation of Facemash.

Zuckerberg appears in the film as a kind of anti-hero, insensitive and calculating, who seems not to care much about the people around him. No one from the Facebook team participated in the film , and, its current CEO, called the script as mere fiction.

Curiosities

With now over 10 years, it is clear that it is already possible to gather a series of curious facts about the social network of one of the most famous CEOs in the world.

Meet some of the most interesting:

1. It is possible to register an heir user of your account

With the option to register the heir user, it is possible to choose a person who will manage your account , in case something happens to you.

The access that this person will have on their profile is limited to the administration of some content, without it being possible to view private information, such as chat conversations, for example.

2. Al Pacino welcoming

When the site still had the name of "thefacebook", when accessing the login page, it was possible to visualize, in the upper screen corner, the face of the actor Al Pacino.

Look:

To this day, there is no justification for why the face of the interpreter of Michael Corleone appeared on the site, but it is known that the image was developed by a colleague from Zuckerberg.

3. The color blue and its relationship with Mark Zuckerberg

Mark has already declared himself colorblind, and for him, the best color is blue. Reason why the CEO decided to introduce the color throughout the site.

4. The languages present

Facebook currently has 70 different language options to be used.

The coolest thing is that, in addition to a wide variety of languages from around the world, there are options such as: "English Upside Down" , where everything that is written is upside down.

And that of "English (Pirate)", an English version with pirate idioms, which replaced the "user name" with "pirate name", "Name" is replaced by "Captain's name", "E-mail" it is replaced by "E-bottle" (Something like E-bottle), due to the stories told about the messages sent in bottles.

5. Hackers

In 2014, the number of invasion attempts counted, registered 600 thousand per day. Hackers tried to access important information such as private messages, photos and other user data.

For this reason, it is necessary to generate a password and also activate Facebook's security options, such as providing an access code when entering your account from a device other than yours.

HOW FACEBOOK WORKS

Facebook is basically divided into two worlds - the world of people and the world of business. That is, it offers two profile options to choose from: personal profile or Fanpage.

Personal profile X Fanpage

The personal profile allows you to interact with your friends, post (images, texts, videos), etc. Fanpage, in turn, is the page of your business, it is the presence of your company within Facebook. The main differences between the two options are found in the following table.

Facebook: Personal profile and Fanpage

Type of use: Personal use and Professional use

Users: They are friends and They are followers

Amount of friends: Limited and Unlimited

Who can manage: Single user and multiple users

Customization options: Basic (avatar and cape)and Advanced (avatar, layer, CTA's and plug-ins)

Posts Allows the sending of individual messages and Allows mass message delivery.

Statistics It does not offer any.

- Offers statistics on Facebook Insights.

- It has special tabs.

- Allows advertisements through Facebook Ads.

The type of profile you choose should be associated with your goal when using Facebook. Below, we detail some of the resources presented in the previous table.

Users

If your profile is personal, other Facebook users can be your friends. What does that mean? It means that if you accept another user as a friend or if you accept as a friend of another user, you will automatically follow him and he will also follow you, which means that both can see each other's posts in the News Feed (constantly list updated with the posts of friends, pages and other connections you have created).

Seeing the publication of your friends in the News Feed, Facebook offers the options to react on the post by giving a "like", "I love it", "it saddens me", "it surprises me". Or it also allows you to comment on your friends' posts or share.

In a Fanpage, other Facebook users can be your followers. This is the type of profile that Facebook itself recommends to companies, public figures, etc.

Users who become followers of a Fanpage, receive all their posts in the News Feed and can react and interact with them.

Amount of friends

In the personal profile you can have a maximum of 5 thousand friends. That is, a maximum of 5,000 people can connect to you. And that's because using a personal profile for brand disclosure is against Facebook's guidelines and terms.

In the Fanpage, the number of followers you can have is unlimited. In addition, the scope of the publications of a Fanpage is much greater. The Fanpage offers resources to boost your posts through an ad, which makes them reach a larger audience.

Customization options

The personalization options of a personal profile are basic: you can customize your cover image, avatar and

URL. The possibility of a personal profile to customize your URL is quite recent. This makes the profile easier to find by other users.

The customization options of a Fanpage are multiple. You can describe your page in the "About" tab. A good description is important, so by adding your site address, you can achieve a good search ranking.

You can customize your URL, making it easier to find by other users. One suggestion is: adopt an exclusive and simple name - that will make the search for your page easier, as well as access to it.

You can change the profile picture, cover page and create avatars.

In a Fanpage, you can also create tabs (plug-ins). So, for example, if you want to offer your followers a free Ebook, you can create a tab called "Ebook" and redirect the user to the page where the Ebook is available. This can also provide you with increased traffic on your blog or website .

Another great Facebook customization tool is in the "Preferred audience for the page" tab. This tab allows you to define your target audience. Who do you want to reach? What is the average age and gender of your audience? What are your main interests? In the last tab of the settings, you can define these and other alternatives, so that your page appears mainly for people who fit the profile defined by you.

Statistics

For those who have a Fanpage, Facebook offers some tools that are not available in personal profiles. This is a combo of tools that includes Facebook Insights and Facebook Ads , as well as some special plug-ins.

Facebook Insights is a tool that allows those who have a Fanpage to know in detail the accumulated statistics of the page. You can find out about the reactions to your posts, about the reach of the page, about the visits to the page, about the actions of the followers on the page, about your posts, about your videos and much more.

Facebook Ads is Facebook's own ad platform. Through it it is possible to disseminate not only advertising of your brand, but also content, materials or any other type of post that you find interesting to reach a larger audience.

With it, you can also create segmented campaigns for those who access that social network and also Instagram. It is possible to make hundreds of combinations of public and interests to reach more people.

Facebook, through the resources it offers to those who own Fanpage, is a great tool for business.

Means

Currently, Facebook presents a series of resources that leave the user experience more complete and also more fun.

On top of that, updates on the site are constant, and from time to time, new resources are added.

We separate the main ones:

1. Customization

When you create a personal page on Facebook, it is possible to customize it according to your preferences, adding a profile picture, which allows others to identify you better, and a cover photo.

In case you have a Fanpage, it is possible to use these resources according to your marketing strategy and the visual identity of your brand.

Do you have any difficulty starting a marketing strategy for your company on Facebook? Learn more in this free E-book that we prepare for you.

2. Add friends

It has the possibility to add and connect with your friends and acquaintances, not only from your city, but from all over the world. This became the great key to social networks, since all of them revolve around the relationship between people.

However, remember that only the pages of people have

this resource. In the Fanpage, instead of friends, you will have followers who will enjoy your page and interact with your posts.

You never create a personal account to disclose your brand or company. In addition to the fact that your personal page has a limited number of friends that can be added, this action violates Facebook guidelines.

3. Chat

Chat is the quick and practical way to communicate not only with your friends, but with other people who are registered on the network.

In it, it is possible to send messages in real time, in addition to sharing images, videos, links, audios, files and send gifs, figurines and the user's current location.

The resource recalls the MSN instant messaging service, which was gradually replaced by other products such as Skype, social media chats and mobile applications such as WhatsApp, which was purchased by Facebook, in 2014.

4. Follow a page

When you like a page, it is possible to accompany the updates and also the news that is published on it.

The interesting thing about Facebook pages is that they give greater visibility to the owner and allow the public to interact directly through comments, likes and messages.

In addition to that, your personal account shows the pages in a row, indicating what your preferences are. It's an optimal way for other people to know you better, right?

We know well that pages are not the only option that can be followed within the social network. The "like" button has already become a registered trademark and can be used as interaction in publications in general.

Recently, other buttons were incorporated into this option, so that the user can express that he loves a certain publication, or if he felt sad when viewing it.

5. Share content

The possibility of sharing content with other people connected to you is probably the greatest interaction within the website.

By sharing a content, you can share information, news, opinions and news to other users.

It is also possible to share photos, personal or not, directly through Facebook, or through integration with Instagram , which was also bought by Mark in 2012.

In the shared contents, it is still possible to mark friends, show the current location and "add an activity", as something you are seeing, as you are feeling, a cause you are supporting or a book you are reading, just to name a few examples .

Recently, a new resource was also added to the selection of status update options.

It is possible to make a live video stream. That is, it is possible to record something that is happening in real time, and users can interact with you. After finishing, your video will remain in your timeline.

6. Applications

Facebook applications are interaction tools that can be games, jokes and tests that are integrated into your account, even abas (windows that appear just below the cover photo) that can help you in your business, within your page.

And when we talk about abas for Fanpage, the options are countless. They range from the personalization of the same, to the generation of leads , through a Like Gate , which shows different content for those who like and for whom not too.

"Tap" button

The "give a touch" option to someone on the social network was never exactly defined. Facebook introduced it as a way to get someone's attention or simply say "Hello" in a less formal way.

The website itself did not create a specific definition for the function and even, they like to leave the option open to everyone's interpretations.

8. Ads

Through the social network itself, it is possible to create paid ads to attract specific audiences, making it more interesting for people who are watching it.

It is also possible to assemble them according to your needs, in addition to the possibility of boosting your company's sales. The campaigns do not have a maximum value and can be readjusted according to the results and demands that appear over time.

Creation of events and groups

Today, the creation of events on Facebook to announce and invite who you want to go to your party, meeting or meeting became almost mandatory.

This resource facilitates the exchange of information about events and also helps in the control of who will attend. It is also possible to create groups for the most diverse purposes, ranging from gathering people with the same musical taste, for example, to grouping people from the same classroom, so that they can discuss past subjects and activities.

Statistics

Facebook statistics have been growing steeply since its inception, and when we talk about it being the most accessed site in the world, we are not lying!

According to this year's data, the social network has 99 billion monthly active users and 89 billion monthly active mobile users. Secondly, we have WhatsApp and thirdly, Instagram .

For this type of data, that is why companies try to be present in this social network so that they can be seen and so that they can disseminate their own brand.

Why use Facebook as a personal tool

Facebook has both prestige and popularity, coupled with an incredible ease of use, which make it virtually inevitable to have to go through this platform when promoting our personal image. Therefore, if you think of using it for professional purposes, as if it were LinkedIn, you are more than right.

Facebook is ideal for networking allowing you to create groups and events not so formal that will allow you another type of approach. Everything will depend on the imprint you want to give. And not only that, but also, if you want to make radical changes or simply disappear to disconnect a little and change your air, all that is already planned. Facebook is, without a doubt, the social network that most understands the user, in it you will find, in addition to means, a good orientation for emerging problems.

Facebook profile

There are several reasons why many people and

companies use the Profile mode and one of them is how you position yourself in front of the audience you intend to reach. The main work we can do with a marketing strategy , using a personal profile on Facebook, is the qualification of leads.

Qualification

Qualifying a lead is, in some way, creating a subtle link that oscillates between the formal and the informal, while there is a minimum of intimacy, we must be careful not to exceed the limits. It will depend a lot on your instinct and intuition and you should never forget that you have to know how to separate the personal from the professional. There are three extremely simple ways to generate and rate leads on Facebook :

Friend requests

Accepting a friend request is synonymous with voluntarily agreeing to receive your messages and view your publications. Of course, much better, still, is when it is the lead who requests your friendship, that can mean an active interest in your proposal. So, either he accepting your request or you accepting his request, in both cases there is an implicit consent that enables you to send content. This consent is the fuel of lead generation . Be careful, do not miss this gesture of trust!

Creating groups you manage

Creating thematic groups is very interesting because it

allows you, in addition to creating nutrition flows, to rotate your list of friends. The group mode accepts more than 5000 contacts, therefore, you can create a group and add your friends list, if one day you need to renew it you can delete some contacts from your personal profile, without fear, because they will continue as members of your group.

Once you have put this group into operation, you can create several types of dynamics, both content and segmentation. Promote debates, conduct surveys, create promotions, inform offers, draw a prize, disseminate news and many other ways to keep your audience growing and engaged.

Creating events that you produce

Events are fundamental, they are like the pillars of an intangible construction. We need events to give materiality to our proposal. Without a doubt, you have already seen someone complaining that many people confirmed presence on Facebook, but that very few were. It does not occur to them to think that the error could have been theirs by having an inadequate expectation of a social network and not having used their resources correctly.

Therefore, do not make the same mistake, although it is possible that a facebook event for some unexplained mystery has the same number, or more, of presences than confirmations, in most cases it is not. We generally expect 10% of the confirmations, because the function of the Facebook event is not, in essence, to disseminate, but to stimulate the imaginary in relation to your venture.

TIPS FOR SUCCESSFUL MARKETING STRATEGY ON FACEBOOK

A marketing mix on the Internet does not work without its branch "social networks". Besides, any social network is more effective than Facebook to develop its brand image (brand building in English), its customer relationships and to manage its reputation.

This is due to the significant number of long-range advertising opportunities offered by the social network. You will only enjoy Facebook as a marketing tool if you are correctly exploiting the potential of its possibilities. Find below 8 marketing tips on Facebook that will help you optimize your social media entry and get the most out of this online channel:

1. The basics of Facebook marketing

The basis of success on Facebook is to set up a professional page . This is why it is advisable to take your time to exploit this page as best as possible. All important information must be indicated first. In addition to the location and opening hours, details such as the product palette or the story of the company's creation may be of interest to users.

A fully completed profile containing relevant information in the background gives an impression of seriousness. Images must also convey professionalism and be of good quality. For profile and cover photos, be careful that your images have an ideal resolution and corresponding dimensions.

2. Coordinate all channels

Successful social network marketing

If you want to use Facebook as an element of your online marketing mix, you should harmonize the different channels used with each other to take advantage of synergy effects and incorporate a link to your corporate website.

These referrals generate social signals (social signals) that are considered important for Google and actually constitute a factor for SEO optimization on search engines. Many comments and a high sharing counter reflect the importance and relevance of a site for users, but also for Google.

The managers of the social networks of the company, commonly called community managers, must be careful that all content can be quickly and easily shared and communicate well on the social networks used. The classic actions are as follows:

- Sharing Buttons (Social Plug-ins)
- Buttons to social networks

- Plugin for managing a Facebook page
- RSS feeds and "favorites and bookmarks" services

3. Do not forget the mobiles

In France, the leader in social networks has 31 million active users each month, 25 million of whom have already connected from a smartphone or tablet. In fact, 80% of French users connect from these mobile devices . Around the world according to the same source, 1.6 billion users connect every day in the first quarter of 2016, including 1.4 exclusively from a mobile .

These figures speak for themselves and reflect the importance of mobile optimization . This also applies to social networks, starting with the layout and images. In this regard, Facebook indicates the exact dimensions for profile and cover photos . Mobile users present alow level of attention on Facebook and can thus decide in a few seconds to scroll down when a content does not interest them. All publications must therefore provide concise and relevant images.

4. Increase the engagement of a community of fans

Is the success of a Facebook page measured by its number of likes (or likes in French)? Not really. A "like" only benefits the company if the user is active. Practices that do not comply with the morality of Facebook marketing, such as the purchase of "likes", are to be avoided. Indeed, the acquisition of a large amount of likes does not increase the scope of your publications so far.

The real goal is to acquire fans and encourage them to interact. Fan engagement increases with relevant content. Whoever keeps current trends and those of a community and reacts accordingly, makes sure to gain new fans and increase the range of its page accordingly. A community can develop very quickly with a snowball effect thanks to the sharing and the different contacts of each active fan, who can become interested or clients.

5. Communication and interaction

Having your own Facebook page is ideal for sharing information and news. On the other hand, we should not use this platform only to deliver information, but especially to set up a dialogue and react to the various questions of the interested parties. If you respond to queries with clear added value, you can build customer loyalty and strengthen your relationship with the company.

We get interaction through contests or polls. In addition, polls bring many benefits: by integrating the fans of your page into the decision process You not only increase the trust they have for the company, but you also gain valuable information about your customers' expectations of the company.

6. The right timing

Good timing

Facebook marketing, by nature, never stops. But thanks to the management tools for existing social networks that allow to post content offline, no employee should stay at his computer permanently. The time aspect, however, plays an important role on Facebook. On the one hand, regularity is important: abandoned pages, on which we have not found new content for years, do not convey an image of seriousness or professionalism. On the other hand, the timing must be fair and a publication should ideally be posted when as many users as possible are connected. Whoever wants to be sure of the numbers can use a tool likeFanpage Karma .

7. Video is the new selfie

Thanks to the introduction of Facebook's new video player (and the automatic play feature), the use of videos on the social platform has become very profitable. Thanks to this, companies quickly gain the attention of their target. Animated images of this kind convey more emotions in communication and they often allow professional representation of products or services. Plus, Facebook is great for spreading viral videos . Two good examples of recent years are the Ice Bucket Challenge or the Harlem Shake.

8. Advertise with Facebook

If you have not managed to naturally get the desired number of fans on your Facebook page, there is still the opportunity to advertise on Facebook . With the help of Facebook-Ads, companies reach their target by showing advertising content in their news feed

HERE'S HOW TO CREATE A POWERFUL FACEBOOK PAGE

Complete the company profile

Go to the "About" section in the left menu and write as much relevant information as you can.

Make sure the contact information (company name, address, phone number) is the same everywhere on social networks. This information must also match those on the company's website.

Name of the page

Make sure the name of your Facebook page matches the name of your company and validate your page to make it the official page of your business.

Category

Add categories relevant to your business area. These categories will allow you to position yourself according to your most important keywords.

username

Create a short representative address so that visitors can easily find your Facebook page. You can as well promote it easily.

Website

Add the address of your website, do not take the risk of losing visitors who want to visit your site or, even worse, lose those who want to buy your products or services.

About

Briefly introduce your organization. Users will be informed about their expectations if they subscribe to your Facebook page. Make sure all your details are complete and up-to-date.

milestones

Tell the story of your company from the perspective of its key moments. By highlighting the most important milestones in your history, you will create a sense of community with your business.

Among the ideas for using milestones, you can post images of your company at the opening, celebrate the good moves of your employees, or promote your product launches.

TIP

OF PRO to attract your most engaged "fans" to your website, add a call to action with a link to your milestones for more information.

Liked pages

Facebook is a place of entertainment, and users who are interested in you want to know what interests you . By loving other pages, you will humanize your business and increase the visibility of your own page and interest in it.

Settings

Allow all your subscribers to post to your Facebook page. You must never forget that Facebook is a social network foremost. It is therefore strongly recommended to leave room for discussion. In addition, a customer comment can tell you a lot about your organization.

To avoid dissatisfaction with users visiting your company's page, make sure to clearly outline the moderation policy that applies to your Facebook page. Tell users what types of behavior or purpose will result in the removal of a message (inciting hatred, verbal abuse, posting sexual content, etc.). Also create text filters to hide specific words that could be found in comments.

TIP OF PRO

Do not delete the publication from an unsatisfied customer. This could especially increase his frustration.

Instead, invite the person to talk to you privately and try to resolve the situation with them. So, not only will you demonstrate the quality of your company's customer service, but you will also avoid the company receiving negative feedback that could hurt its image.

OPTIMIZE POSTS ON YOUR FACEBOOK PAGE

For your Facebook marketing to reach the target, visitors to your business page must provide relevant content for the user. As there are no two users or two identical business pages, it is important to vary your marketing actions on Facebook.

Frequency of publications

Adapt the frequency of your publications according to the type of content and the degree of effort that their production has requested. Consider doing 3 to 5 publications a week, but do not post the same content multiple times.

Do some tests. Try to maximize the clicks and engagement of your target audiences by varying the number of posts per week.

Types of publications

It is very important to vary the type of content you will publish. To achieve this, here is a list, by type of publications, to add to your monthly publication program.

- Make 1 publication linked to your blog;
- Ask your audience 1 question to stimulate discussion;
- Create 1 to 3 non-promotional publications;
- Share 1 to 3 publications related to the content of your brand;
- Share 1 to 3 useful articles from influencers in your industry;
- Publish 1 to 2 videos, depending on your resources. Feel free to post videos found on the web;
- Take 15 minutes each day to answer questions and comments.
- Observe your results. Then, vary the types based on the publications that brings you the best click through rates and the strongest commitment.

Length of publications

Make publications containing 100 to 500 words. Messages that are too short do not receive the same commitment as those whose content is long enough to give readers the urge to click to find out more.

Hours and days of publications

Know your audience Depending on the family or work situation of your "fans" or any other factor, your best time to post content is likely to vary. Check by trial what are the best days and hours and concentrate your publications in these periods.

Hashtags (#)

Participate in great hashtag -themed web-based discussions or start new ones! This will increase your visibility to the relevant hashtags users who might find you interesting. To learn more about "Hashtags" see our article #Hashtags 101 .

Image quality

Whenever possible, avoid using royalty free images (stock photos). Use original images. Create your own visuals Facebook users prefer the original content.

Make sure, when preparing your marketing strategy on Facebook, to provide time for research and taking photos.

Take advantage of Facebook advertising

Facebook is certainly the most powerful advertising platform to date. Use it to complement your marketing initiatives. Here are the best practices to follow for Facebook advertising

Avoid the button "Put the publication forward"; use Power Editor instead to promote your publications

Avoid-the-button-boost post-put-in-front-marketing-facebook

The reason is simple: this button optimizes your publication for engagement only. Therefore, if the goal of your Facebook ad is to redirect visitors to your website with a publication with a link, you will not be able to optimize it to generate as many clicks as possible.

NB .: See the recent Facebook update that integrates Power Editor into Ads Manager

Install the conversion pixel on your website

Prioritize conversions that bring you revenue. By installing the conversion pixel , you'll benefit from remarketing and optimizing conversions from your ads.

Promote publications that work best

Some of your publications could become viral, and if you are lucky, they will be aligned with your business goals.

If such a thing happens, promote the publication without fail! You will see that it will get a very large reach at low cost. Remember this rule: the quality and interest that people bring to your publication has a high impact on the visibility that Facebook gives it.

Improve the relevance rating of your ads

Follow the relevance index closely. The principle is simple. The higher the relevance rating of your ads, the less expensive your ads will be.

Increase the likes

Increase the likes on your page by inviting users who are interested in the posts you have posted.

Evaluate the performance of your page

The time to want as much as possible as possible is over. Only a minority of your "fans" will see your posts. Remember that the main goal of your Facebook marketing is to increase the turnover of your business.

HERE ARE SOME IDEAS OF PERFORMANCE INDICATORS TO ANALYZE:

Scope, interactions and engagement rate

Follow the scope of your page and the interactions it generates to assess your health. Calculate the engagement rate by dividing the number of interactions by the scope of the page.

Understand the type and timing of the best performing publications. By keeping these indicators in your dashboard, you will learn to satisfy your audiences and improve the performance of your page.

Clicks to your website and conversions

For the majority of companies, the website is a potentially effective tool for earning income, but only if you know how to use it well.

To make the most of your site, it is important that you increase the number of visits and that those from Facebook complement the actions you want to see accomplished. Start by setting up conversions for your website using the Facebook conversion pixel or Google Analytics goals .

google analytics dashboard

Then, evaluate which types of posts bring you the most clicks and the most conversions.

Action button

Assign a value to clicks on the action button. Here's how to evaluate the value of the action button.

Take the example of a call button. Calculate the total value of sales by phone. Divide this amount by the number of calls. Then multiply the result by the number of clicks on the button.

Number of emails acquired

By tracking your website, evaluate the performance of your Facebook page in terms of acquired contacts. An email will allow you to directly contact your potential customers and target more precisely your Facebook ads.

Sales

Of course, calculating Facebook sales directly is the best way to evaluate the performance of your page. This requires a somewhat more complex configuration. Feel free to call an agency if you want to do a thorough analysis of your sales from the Web and Facebook marketing.

Do not forget that Facebook marketing has benefits that are not limited to direct sales. Do not be too quick to condemn a Facebook page that does not seem to bring you the anticipated income.

FACEBOOK MARKETING: GUIDE TO GET CUSTOMERS AND SALES WITH A SMALL BUSINESS

Who doesn't have Facebook today? Look around and look for that "weirdo" that does not yet use this social network (it will cost you to find it).

With that huge volume of users, there is also a huge volume of potential customers. Many businesses are already taking advantage of the platform to grow, get an intimate relationship with their followers and sell.

1 Facebook for startup businesses: it all starts with a fan page

Using Facebook for small businesses means having an already defined content strategy, the first step for a business is to set up a Fan Page (fan page) because this is the type of page Facebook recommends for business.

On the one hand you will have your profile for the private management of your contacts, but for everything that is your business the correct step is to set up a Fan page . Doing so is very easy: you can directly visit Facebook Pages and there you can register a page.

You will have to design two images:

Main image: it is the image that will appear when someone searches for the page and the highlighted one that your business will represent on Facebook. A size of 180 × 180 px is ideal for this image.

Cover Image: this will be the picture that will feature at the top of your Fan Page. It's great to do ads, redirect traffic, or get exposure to a specific subject. The perfect size is 851 x 315 px.

My recommendation is that you put a picture of yourself in the main image and explain how to contact you in your blog or in other places where you can be present through the cover.

2 The landing page

When people arrive at a wall where there are many comments, many contents, they are a little lost and do not know very well what they have to do.

Instead of bringing the new views directly to the wall -

people who are not yet your fan - you can also create a Landing page and mark it as the default page.

In this case, the visits of people who are not your fans will end on your Landing page, a page specifically designed for the user to become a fan before starting a relationship with your online presence on Facebook.

To set up your landing page you can use an application called Static HTML tab and that allows you to develop a professional presence on Facebook. Through this totally free application you can define two views: a first view for people who are not Fan and another for people who are Fan.

#3 What content should you use on Facebook?

Basically, the first thing you need to do is mention new posts you wrote on your blog. Do it manually, generate your own posts a few days a week, based on how you've described the blog's editorial calendar.

You can also ask questions (there is a feature called Questions) which is very useful for your fans to get reviews on.

They can also share photos, videos and this is very useful for all physical companies such as restaurants, stores, but also for B2B (business to business) businesses. For example, it occurs to me that presenting a printing press ' digital machines can be very valuable, in photos or on video.

Most businesses are not making ample use of these tools that are actually useful and allow us to offer a glimpse of what's behind, what companies are selling and that's very optimistic.

You should share links and I recommend that you not only post your own links, but also that if an article has been written in a journal that you think is worth highlighting for people following you... Do it, don't just share your resources!

Attempt not to be very formal, so don't frighten the friends. Be human, talk about things personal and amusing. In short, be no pain.

How many times you have to do it each day?

Those you want. You usually realize that the more active you are on Facebook, the greater the benefit you usually get to this network. Nor is it about becoming a spammer: everything depends on your ability to add value (I usually do it twice a day at the most).

Very often, when I look at small business ventures on Twitter, the topic of the post is the one that sins the most. They're having difficult time letting go and not writing like in a sales brochure.

It's just about sustaining a professional relationship that continues for ever. Chat with one of your customers when you drink a coffee or eat. That client has become a friend over time and you don't always talk about work with friends, right?

Any more nothing less. See how easy that is? We continue to develop your future plan on Facebook with this exclusive Facebook guide for small businesses.

What tools can I use to easily and quickly create the content?

Non-designers are given numerous designer tools. Many software that will help you create content without having to expend too much time or completing a complete Photoshop course.

These are recommended:

- Canva : the best known tool for creating content for any social network. Enter, register and you can create the cover, profile picture, Facebook Ads ads and publications by dragging photos and editing text.
- Pablo : Do you just want a nice phrase and a nice background? Try Pablo, Buffer's quintessential tool for creating more content.
- PicMonkey: collages, filters, photo edits and all that is needed for photos.
- Recite : if you don't like Pablo's photos, Recite is your choice. Write a quote or phrase and choose from the numerous templates to create your phrases in seconds.

#4 How to get more engagement on your Fan Page

Another very interesting business resource is Facebook Ads, an online advertising platform in which you have two types of commodities: one is traditional advertising and the other is sponsored.

Both goods have the idea of making your own Fan page or external website available and aim to get more fans or link to a landing page that you've made. Facebook ads is fairly cheap, and has an exceptionally good segmentation capability.

You can segment on geographical location criteria, socioeconomic level, sex, topics of interest, you can segment by "Friends of your fans," you can do a lot of things and I really recommend, if you are a small business, launch a 5 or 10 euro campaign a day (you can control the budget you spend) because it can bring a lot of value to your business.

Ok, if you're a solo entrepreneur, think about Facebook ads so you can expand within this social network in your "distance." For example, developing a Landing page would be an interesting strategy, where you are offering to register your newsletter, a document or a mini-course.

In this scenario, depending on the subscribers who subscribe to your Facebook newsletter, you can track the impact of your promotion on Facebook, which helps you to set a cost per subscription that is a very useful measure for tracking, more interesting That cost per click on your ad.

#5 You spend money with the idea of growing your database of potential clients on an online advertising campaign. An opportunity rather than a cost, yet another case in favor of keeping a small business operation on Facebook Where can I view my Facebook statistics?

Facebook Insigths is Google Analytics counterpart but within Facebook. It's your page's analytics section and it's interesting to know a little about the stuff that's going on there: see the most popular posts Learn a little more about the user profile that connects with your content Learn how new users hit your landing page or wall See which sites they visit Know what external connections get you more clicks and more fans Anyway, a sequence

Like any boss, to make your decisions, you need the details. Facebook Insights is your unique, small business Facebook scorecard.

#6 Expand Social Widgets on Facebook These social Facebook widgets virtually serve to illustrate the behavior you can have on Facebook in your blog. There are several types of widgets: one of them is the "Like" button, recently completed with an option to send to the user group of Facebook.

These two buttons are very valuable and we

recommend that you integrate them into your blog so that users can easily share content.

Another popular widget is an activity feed that displays the face of a blog follower and invites non-fans to page fans.

As you can see, the conversation is added to the conversation. If you introduce these resources on your blog, your audience can grow on Facebook as well as on Facebook. People prefer to read content directly on Facebook. Facebook is a time-consuming platform.

Think about these resources that Facebook offers for free and integrate social information into your blog.

The third widget I want to comment on is the Facebook comment thread. This allows you to leave comments on posts you publish on your blog, but you can use your Facebook profile directly.

With this plugin, conversation threads are developed through comments made on Facebook. This is very positive and a very good alternative to spam in comments.

There is a re-effect of the conversation between your blog and Facebook. This is a positive effect. Please try to use it.

7 advanced use on Facebook

One is the use of the Facebook application. If you have

the money to invest and have a good idea, developing your own application for Facebook is a great way to gain business visibility and become more accessible. fan. The application needs to know that it can access a lot of profile data for users who are fans of this application. You can also know more data about the users who use it.

Of course, this has significant development and integration costs, but it also has great business value.

I think it 's suitable for many businesses, not freelancers or people who start alone or have just launched a business, but for a restaurant for example, integrating an application to reserve tables can be of great interest or that people share their cocktails Favorites with the bar where they will spend time.

8 Turn your fans into subscribers

A Facebook fan is somewhat volatile. He is just one step away from keeping in touch with you, and even your fans can only see 7% of your posts.

Isn't it a very sad statistic?

For this reason, try to collect as much traffic as possible from your Facebook page to your blog or website. Then you need to make your fan a subscriber by email. This way, you can always contact your fans the way you want.

9 Throw yourself now

You don't need anything else to start working with Facebook. Follow these steps and your community will gradually grows around the page. You will bring in more confidence and your followers and clients will feel you as a more intimate company.

And if you like this Facebook marketing guide for small businesses, I will ask you in return.

Just never pass it to the competition.

HOW TO MAKE MONEY ON FACEBOOK PAGE

With more than 1 billion users, Facebook is a great opportunity for businesses that want to use Facebook as a sales or advertising tool. But the question that many people ask is is it possible to generate income on this social network without having a company?

Is there a way to start making money on the Facebook page if I don't have a business? There is no way: there are 5 different ways to do it! Requirements for monetizing Facebook pages

The first essential requirement is clearly having a Facebook page. Several readers have asked if they can make money with their Facebook profile. And the answer is yes.

However, since personal profiles are not specific, it is much more difficult to monetize personal profiles than Facebook pages. Your Facebook profile can include friends with completely different interests. Some people like techno music, others like rock and pop.

Some people have pets, others don't like animals. On the other hand, Facebook pages are more specific because fans have the same common interest.

When creating a page about rock music, only those who like rock music click "Like". If your page is aimed at pet owners, only people with dogs, cats, or parakeets will be fans of it.

So the first thing to keep in mind is that you need to have your own Facebook page. Forget to make money using your personal profile on this social network. Remember that you can now create ads on Facebook.

1. Make money on Facebook with mentions

If you have a lot of fans following a Facebook page publication, you can make money by mentioning or promoting your company, company, or anyone who wants to know you.

Many small businesses, brands, or even entrepreneurs don't exist on Facebook or have their own pages, and they want to increase visibility among users. That's why they pay pages to many fans featured in Facebook posts (with photos) to attract customers and increase visits to web pages.

To achieve this type of collaboration, you can search for Facebook or Google companies interested in your page, create the most relevant lists, contact them, and reach an economic agreement in exchange for publication Is the best.

But be careful: do not contact anyone. You need to do it with companies and brands related to Facebook page themes and interests. If you have a mobile phone page, it's not logical to mention a food company, for example. Ideally, contact a brand that sells accessories and products related to mobile phones.

2. Sell your own products

One of the easiest ways to make money on Facebook pages is to sell your own digital products. These include e-books you write, such as e-books, guides and manuals, online courses you create, articles that you can download immediately as mp3 music.

To sell them, simply upload these files to a mega or other storage platform and post an attractive photo with a brief description and payment link on Facebook. If you repeat frequently on Facebook pages, fans should feel free to saturate with ads, so don't look into this type of post. It is recommended that you publish one of these promotional posts for every 10 regular posts.

3. Promote affiliate products on the page

Do you have your own product? Then you sell other people's items and receive a commission for every sale you get. This is called "affiliate marketing".

This method works exactly the same as the previous method. Instead of adding a link to the product, you need to publish the affiliate link provided by the registered company.

There are many companies that have affiliate programs: Clickbank, Amazon, Apple, Zalando, Asos. Search the Internet for the best company for Facebook pages, sign up for its affiliate program, and select products related to your fans. Publish an affiliate link and receive a total commission each time someone clicks on that link and buys a product.

CHAPTER THREE

INSTAGRAM MARKETING 2020

Defining an Instagram marketing strategy is the first step for anyone who wants to use this network to promote a company or even their personal brand. With the growth of this network in Brazil, many brands have been looking for Instagram as an alternative for the promotion of their products and services.

Fashion, food, beauty and tourism, for example, are sectors that can not be left out of Instagram, because they are the "face" of this network and therefore, find in it a great place to get leads.

The big problem is that many of these brands are moving to Instagram marketing, still in an amateurish, makeshift fashion. In a market as competitive as social media marketing, treating a corporate Instagram account the same way you treat your personal account is a true strategic suicide.

It is therefore important that the brand first of all prepare itself by devising a marketing strategy on Instagram, before going around publishing anything and praying for some result. We all know that this does not work.

- Understanding the concept
- Understanding Instagram Marketing
- Determining Your Instagram Goals
- Content Development
- Structure preparation
- Alignment with other strategies
- Results monitoring
- You will find that this basic planning of a digital marketing strategy on Instagram is not as difficult as it may seem, but it is certainly critical for the brand to achieve good results.

The walkthrough for crafting an Instagram marketing strategy

Below you will see the step by step to work out a digital marketing strategy on Instagram and design your company, or personal brand in this tool.

1 - Understanding the concept

The first step in building an Instagram marketing strategy is to understand the very concept of social media marketing, which has very different characteristics from other digital marketing strategies.

Social media marketing is relationship-based, meaning you first build rapport with your followers and fans, and then subtly present your business proposition. So this is a medium strategy and so you need to start now and then reap the rewards later. There is no immediate result in social media marketing.

2 - Understanding Instagram Marketing

The marketing on Instagram , whether personal or corporate, subject to its own rules and understand these rules and network characteristics is essential to your marketing strategy.

Instagram is by definition an entertainment medium. Therefore, your business approach should be to display, that is, to be in the right place for the right people, without interfering with the natural conversation of the network.

3 - Determine Your Instagram Goals

As with any other social media platform, when designing an Instagram marketing strategy you must clearly determine what your main goals are with your brand presence on this channel.

The marketing on Instagram does not work or works very little in some situations, such as direct selling, for example. Therefore, your proposal should be to create an alternative to your other online marketing strategies.

By clearly determining your goals, you will be able to select your metrics and make a really technical measurement of the results. It is not for any other reason that in our Instagram Course , we put this issue right between the first training modules.

4 - Develop exclusive content for Instagram

Another interesting feature of Instagram is that it is extremely demanding in terms of content. In our social media marketing course, I always say that content is the main tool in this area, and Instagram would be no different.

A marketing strategy on Instagram differs greatly from people using the tool. While in private use, we do not have much concern with the sequence of actions, in the case of corporate use, everything needs to be thought of.

This is why it is important that you study the posts of companies in your area that stand out on Instagram to understand your competition and also to see how your audience reacts to these posts.

Images - Always work with unique and innovative images. No need to go around taking beaten images to put in your publications, because they don't work, just because they are already "part of the landscape".

Texts - Invest heavily in creating interaction-generating text, with thought-provoking link baits and strong call-to-action, so that your posts can achieve their goal of building rapport with their followers.

Hastags - Hashtags play a major role within an Instagram marketing strategy, so create your own to achieve greater reach and also monitor the most popular hastags.

Content is largely responsible for interactions on Instagram, so believing that the brand can succeed in this area without proper care in pre-preparing this content is a waste of time.

5 - Prepare your structure

Instagram, even more so than other social media like Facebook and Twitter, is a conversation environment, so you will need to have an interaction structure, otherwise all your efforts to create an Instagram marketing strategy will be wasted.

People comment and ask questions in your publications, and it is very important for you to create the relationship ties we mentioned in the first item of this article that you are ready to interact with these comments and questions.

The person responsible for these interactions will need to be fully aligned with the Instagram Marketing strategy designed by your team, otherwise the conversion potential of these interactions may be lost, or worse the brand may end up in a social media crisis

6 - Align your Instagram marketing strategy with Facebook's

We all know that Facebook is fully integrated with Instagram, so it makes perfect sense to align your

Instagram marketing strategy with your Facebook marketing strategy to create a digital marketing synergy between them.

Not that you will replicate everything you do on Instagram, in the Facebook interface, which would be a big mistake, but to make these two tools interact with each other, aiming to enhance each one of them.

7 - Set up a good monitoring system

There is only one way for you to analyze the success of an Instagram marketing strategy, as with any other type of online campaign: Building a good conversion tracking strategy.

One of the major problems with Instagram is precisely the lack of links in paid publications, they are only allowed in ads. As a result, most Google Analytics-based traffic monitoring techniques, such as UTM Tagging, are greatly compromised.

Therefore, you will need to create a differentiated tracking system through specific Landing Pages sent in response to your interactions so you can track incoming leads generated on Instagram in your conversion funnel.

HOW TO CUSTOMIZE YOUR INSTAGRAM?

KEY ELEMENTS ON YOUR PROFILE

Have you opened an Instagram account? You can immediately take care of a very simple thing, even before starting to post your first photos: customize your profile.

This is often one of the first elements that will see potential subscribers, so it plays a key role to make a good impression. But how to customize his Instagram? In this article, I will tell you about the five essential elements to inform for the first impression to be positive!

Overview of an Instagram Profile

If you look at an Instagram profile, you will find that it is composed as follows:

Instagram profile: 5 important elements

INSTAGRAM PROFILE: 5 IMPORTANT ELEMENTS

1. There is a user name . It is thanks to this name that other members of Instagram will be able to mention you, it is also the name which will appear in the URL of your profile. For example, I am @salutbyebyeblogwhen I am mentioned and https://www.instagram.com/salutbyebyeblog/when I quote the URL of the profile.

2. There is also a profile picture , most of the time a logo, a picture of the person who manages the account

or a photo symbolizing the main theme of the account.

3. Then there is the name of the account (separate from the username): it is a name a little more marketing, which we see in particular in the search results Instagram.

4. The fourth important element is the Instagram bio , some lines of biography to put forward your account.

5. The last element is the link you include in your Instagram profile, which will be clickable.

Business accounts have a few additional options, which I will return to at the end of this article.

These elements can be modified by clicking on the button "Modify the profile" , which gives access to this screen on mobile:

Edit Instagram Profile

EDIT INSTAGRAM PROFILE

1. Your username

This is one of the first things you have to choose to customize your Instagram.

If you have a website, be aware that the rules for choosing an Instagram user name which amounts to also choosing a domain name .

A name that does not have spaces

A name which, ideally, does not contain characters too complex to memorize (points, underscores, useless numbers, doubled letters as in "elisabeeeeth" ...).

A name that takes your "brand" if you have a blog or you are present on several social networks, It makes memorizing easier.

A name that can be up to 30 characters while knowing that it is better not to fully exploit this limit and opt for a shorter name

And if the username is already taken

You can use a tool like Namechk to see at a glance if a name is available on Instagram as a domain name and on different social networks.

This is also the most common problem encountered: the Instagram user name you would like is already taken . More frustrating still, it is sometimes used by an inactive account, which seems to be abandoned.

To date, Instagram does not offer a miracle solution: it simply advises you to choose a variant of the username you have in mind.

The alternative is to contact yourself the profile you want to retrieve the name: by private courier, by e-mail if the person provides a contact address in the bio of his profile, or by a third party site (search on Google the name of the Instagram profile, the person may have mentioned it on a blog or other site that it manages).

If it is an inactive account, chances are you will receive no response. It may also happen that you are asked for a sum of money in exchange for the release of the desired username: it is up to you to assess whether it is worth it, and to assess the risk of a scam (nothing prevents the person from taking the money without releasing the account later).

Instagram

Even in the case of brands, Instagram remains quite protective vis-à-vis its users. If someone uses a name that is a registered trademark , you can not necessarily get it back. You have to prove that the person is using your brand in a misleading way that could mislead members of the social network.

If this is your case, go to this page , choose "I have a question about usernames" then "My request is for a business account" and then "This username is used by someone else and I can see its content when I access the web address "and finally" I wish to report an infringement of my trademark ".

Change or change the user name

The username can be changed along the way, remember it is a pretty heavy decision: indeed, the username will change where it appears on the Instagram app itself (mentions, comments, etc) but there will be no redirection of links posted to your profile outside the network (ex: websites that mention your account).

You can customize the Instagram username by clicking "Edit Profile" at the "User Name" line. The change is instantaneous.

Get a verified badge on Instagram

Some accounts have a small "Verified Account" blue badge next to their name. It is a badge attributed by Instagram to public figures, celebrities or well-known brands, which attests that this is their official account and not an impostor, as here in the official account of the Game Of Thrones series :

Verified account with blue badge on Instagram

VERIFIED ACCOUNT WITH BLUE BADGE ON INSTAGRAM

A known personality or brand can make a verification request by going to the "Settings" menu of Instagram, then in "Account" and finally in " Request verification" . All you will give is a proof of identity (official ID if you are a natural person, tax return or statute if you are a company).

Instagram verification request

INSTAGRAM VERIFICATION REQUEST

2. Customize your Instagram with a profile picture

The Instagram profile photo is an important part of your identity: it is displayed on your profile, in 110 × 110 pixels format in general. It is preferable, for a good quality display, to put it online in a higher resolution (at least 180 × 180 pixels).

You can choose a nice portrait of you, your logo or an image that perfectly embodies the theme of your account. If you are present on several social networks, it is often relevant to use the same visual everywhere to be more recognizable.

If your logo does not fit in a square, nothing prevents you from choosing only its graphic part , without text, if it is sufficiently recognizable ... Nespresso thus content with the "N" instead of the full brand name.

Nespresso on Instagram

NESPRESSO ON INSTAGRAM

We can also opt for a more compact version of the logo , as do Galeries Lafayette, which transforms their complete logo into a sober "GL" on Instagram, while respecting their graphic identity.

Galeries Lafayette on Instagram

GALERIES LAFAYETTE ON INSTAGRAM

It is often quite relevant to have a profile picture consistent with the general tone of the Instagram account (for example, applying the same type of settings if it's a photo).

3. The name of the Instagram account

As I told you at the beginning of the article, this is the name "marketing" of your account. It will appear on your profile, of course, but also in the Instagram search results if your account has the opportunity to appear there ... It must not exceed 30 characters.

Instagram Search Results

INSTAGRAM SEARCH RESULTS

Initially, I made the mistake of repeating the name of my blog alone ... but in reality, it is advisable to use this space to include keywords relevant to your theme, much like you would on the homepage of a website, in the title tag , in a referencing perspective .

We can either do it in addition to its brand name (which is repeated twice, in the username and in the account name), or completely get rid of the brand name and post only a name descriptive account .

This is the example of the Petit Bison children's decoration brand, with an explicit account name, "Children's Deco".

Little Bison on Instagram

LITTLE BISON ON INSTAGRAM

4. Customize your Instagram bio

The Instagram biography is just a few lines of text, which has the power to attract the attention of a passing visitor! 150 characters to exploit at best to convince!

The idea of the bio Instagram is above all to explain what you offer on your account. Who are you and why would you suddenly decide to follow you?

You can use hashtags (which will be clickable) and emojis . However, e-mail addresses and URLs will not be clickable even if you can add more. Feel free to skip lines to make your message clearer and readable.

A good bio Instagram shows your personality while explaining what you do. It can consist of a few sentences to deliver a complete message ... but also a few points in the form of a list if you share unrelated information.

The Instagram biography can for example include ...

What you offer (type of content, products, theme, activity);

Where you are

One way to contact you

Practical information (eg for a shop, specify where you deliver);

Another account that is important to you (second Instagram account, YouTube profile, etc);

A call to action (download an application, visit a blog, use a specific hashtag to share photos, etc.).

Emojis can be used wisely to save space in your biography: for example, use a flag to indicate your location instead of writing "Location: France"; use an envelope to highlight your contact information, etc.

Here is for example the bio Instagram account "A piece of cake" which offers high-end pastries. At a glance, you can find all the information you need to know : the activity; a contact address; a way to find out more; the places of delivery; the identity of the two pastry chefs who count.

Instagram account A piece of cake

INSTAGRAM ACCOUNT A PIECE OF CAKE

5. The Instagram profile link

At the bottom of the biography, Instagram allows you to add a URL . This is the only place on the social network as I write where the URL is clickable.

So you can use this space ... knowing that you do not have to include a link to your site's homepage at all. You can for example ...

Put the URL of your last article (we can modify the

URL as often as necessary, so many bloggers choose to add their most recent content).

Put the URL of your news of the moment (for example, a new collection in the case of a fashion brand).

Put a URL type Linktree : it is a URL that will refer to a dedicated page, with a menu to access all your important content. That's what Galeries Lafayette do, and here's their Linktree page:

Linktree for Instagram

LINKTREE FOR INSTAGRAM

Put a URL to a landing page dedicated to your Instagram followers on your blog.

Put a URL to creative content: your last YouTube video for example.

Put a URL to an action that is important to you: for example, a newsletter sign-up page, a donation page if you have an association or project to support, etc.

I advise you to use an "explicit" link rather than a non-personalized code link, like zoup.la/ezr439zea5. It makes you want to click when we know (roughly) where we will arrive! Also check that the page you are referring to appears on mobile ... because even if there is a desktop version of Instagram, the site is primarily used on smartphone.

Do not forget also an important element: your URL will be displayed just below your biography. It means that you can use the last line of the Instagram bio to encourage action on your link, put it in context.

And also for business accounts

To customize your Instagram when you have a business account, you have additional options, accessible by clicking on the button "Edit profile".

The Instagram category

It is visible only on the application, not on the desktop version of the site. It allows to indicate to which sector you belong , thus avoiding to repeat it in the bio Instagram itself.

Among these categories, there are either typologies of profiles (for example "Personal Blog", "Cruiser", "Local Company"), or themes ("Travel and Transportation", "Sports and Recreation" for example).

Communication options

As a professional, you can include contact information about your business: e-mail address, phone number, business address. This can also free space in your biography because these coordinates will be displayed directly on your profile as a call-to-action .

A call-to-action contact on Instagram

A CALL-TO-ACTION CONTACT ON INSTAGRAM

A call-to-action

Since we are talking about call-to-action, beyond the contact information, Instagram offers you, in the menu "Communication Options" after clicking on "Edit profile", to display an action button .

This time, it is a button related to different booking services (Appointments by Facebook, Eventbrite, OpenTable, TheFork, Yelp, etc.).

Customize your Instagram account to get started

When you come to customize your Instagram through these key elements , we already put all the chances on his side to deliver a clear message to people who will fall on the profile.

TIPS TO GETTING FOLLOWERS ON INSTAGRAM

Since Instagram has been acquired by Facebook, it is increasingly difficult to develop an account because the social network has implemented an algorithm that reduces the visibility of publications. But there are "good practices" that, in my opinion, will never be harmful!

Win Subscribers on Instagram: Classic Rules of the Social Network First, there is a simple principle on

Instagram as on other social networks: to win subscribers, you need to get interested in the network. Okay, really get involved. I note that often, because of lack of time (or because of laziness, it has to be admitted), I just like the images that fly before my eyes without actually making an effort to write a comment, to go in search of new accounts...

However, it is indeed when one is involved that one derives the most advantages in terms of visibility!

As a social network, Instagram receives the same types of advice as other networks: carefully complete your biography and choose a profile picture; do not flood subscribers with low value added photos; take advantage of the social functions of the network: be interested in others while respecting the ethical principles that we know well (sincerity, no advertising of the type' I follow' Some use the network just to share their daily lives with friends and family (and often have private accounts where they only accept those they know), others-this is my case-also use them to uncover talented artists, to imagine in front of stunning locations, to search decorative ideas...

Tips that work to get more followers on Instagram Original and insightful content Instagram remains a network of "beautiful images." It can be blamed for fostering a cult of excellence, but most of the accounts that grow rapidly and well are those that post quality content.

These are cool pictures, not usually shot with the last but still well framed SLR, not blurred...

A story to tell, I also think, after a few years spent on this network, that people appreciate hearing a unique and personal "voice" behind a (beautiful) image.

Share an anecdote, a life scene, some stories to feed his account, to get a little cold out of the "picture book." It's not easy to keep a certain discretion, but I'm sure it works.

Make your account known that Instagram is a network at the heart of your digital life. And in order to have more followers, you have to give it a place: promote your Instagram account on your blog (through an icon or by embedding any images in your articles), relay your Instagram photos on your Facebook page, build connections between the sites that you run so that we know the presence of your account, include your account in your newsletter...

Nothing also prevents you from pressing your account more explicitly, by posting a message on your blog or on another network to encourage people to join you on Instagram. This year, I did it 2 or 3 times and it helped me to win a couple of dozens of subscribers.

Exploit hashtags and geolocation According to a 2015 report by Dan Zarrella, analyzing nearly 1.5 million Instagram photos, adding hashtags on his pictures raises both the number of likes and the number of comments. Like Twitter, hashtags make it easy to find all the photos related to the same theme.

I discovered very recently that the practice I used was detrimental to my account: like many people, I don't want to "parasitize" the legend of my photo by posting 25 hashtags! And I decided to share in a comment my list of hashtags. Today, I have the impression that I gain more subscribers by limiting myself to a few hashtags and integrating them directly into the legend of the photo.

After several months of stagnating with the same number of followers, this helped my account to start winning again.

You can also allow the geolocation of your images. As a result, they will be more easily linked to a specific location when a person searches for information on the place in question (city, restaurant, trade, etc.), an additional way to gain visibility.

Use Instagram filters According to another Yahoo Labs / Georgia Tech study, filter-based photos are 21 percent more likely to be viewed and 45 percent more likely to receive comments than filter-free photos. According to the report, "the rise in contrast and brightness has a favorable effect on the number of views and comments." The same is true with retouching, which raises the temperature of the object by making it colder.

On the other hand, rising exposure appears to have a negative, though slight, effect on the opinions, even though it is positive for the comments. This goes back to Dan Zarrella's claim that low-saturation images earned 598 percent more than brightly colored pictures! In the same way, the bright photos collected 592 percent more like the dark photos.

At the end of the day, members of the social network choose filters or retouching that enhance the picture without distorting the filters that turn the image. We remain at this level in the search for authenticity.

For my part, I no longer use the filters offered by Instagram, I prefer to manually change some settings (especially contrast / sharpness) to improve the rendering of my photos... But I'm avoiding the heavy editing that's too much of the original photo.

Chat with your subscribers

This is a point on which I still lack investment, recognize it :) If I think to like the comments that I receive or to answer with a small message when the commentary allows, there is one thing that I do little and works well on Instagram: work well your legends !

Photo captions provide a unique opportunity to share trivia, ask questions to your subscribers, tell stories. It creates a link and it's effective for engaging in a discussion.

As on a blog, we can test different things: short legends, long legends, ask a question, explicitly encourage subscribers to comment (according to Dan Zarrella, this explicit dimension would promote interactions).

Keep a coherence

Again, this is not always an easy point to respect ... but for the subscribers (or members of the network who discover you) find it there, it is better that your account releases a certain coherence , that it is in the contents that you post, in your interactions with your subscribers, in your publication frequency.

As on a blog, there is not necessarily an ideal publication frequency but many studies suggest posting several times a week to increase its commitment.

Post at the right time

Instagram no longer displays photos chronologically but highlights posts based on what you are likely to like. Nevertheless, the timing is important because the commitment you receive from the publication plays a lot on the visibility that the social network will give your photo (same on Facebook for me!).

Try to find out when your community is present : rather the evening after dinner, the morning before going to work, on the lunch break, during regular business hours? It can vary from one community to another, which is why I am always dubious when a study announces "ideal publication times"

HOW TO CREATE AN INSTAGRAM MARKETING STRATEGY FOR YOUR BUSINESS

Today, visuals have never been more numerous - be it a quick selfie of our lunch date or the latest video of our pet doing an amazing trick.

This increase in visual content flooding social networks is therefore even more pronounced on Instagram .

As a result, several brands are integrating Instagram into their strategy for growing their business. Videos, gifts and photos generate high engagement rates. If Instagram has become so important, it's because it creates a global social network by connecting people only through visuals, making it a powerful way to capture and hold people's attention.

In recent years, marketers and brands have been trying to capitalize on this monumental growth of Instagram. It has been proven that promoting your business on Instagram is a daunting tool if you learn the tricks to sell your brand on Instagram.

Instagram not only allows you to connect with people and gain visibility, but also paves the way for your brand to be recognized and trusted by Instagram users.

Here are some statistics that show that Instagram is a

powerful platform for brand loyalty:

- In 2017, about 70.7% of all US businesses are on Instagram. That's almost twice as much as in 2016 (48.8%), and this was largely influenced by the inclusion of Instagram profiles in the business.

- 65% of all top performing Instagram posts involve products. Despite the fact that it's not good to promote yourself every time, Instagram users like to look at product photos from time to time. In fact, photos / videos of celebrities / influencers (29%) and lifestyle photos / videos (43%) are behind product images and videos.

- 7 out of 10 hashtags are tagged on Instagram. Hashtags not only help social media users to classify and organize content, but they have also played a key role in creating some of the most successful marketing campaigns.

You must now leverage this client source and use Instagram marketing to grow your business. To sponsor content on Instagram, you must have a Facebook page and use a corporate Instagram profile. Once these two preliminary operations are completed, you must configure your form, define its budget and finally publish it. Here are the steps to follow to create your strategy.

1: Start with a compelling Instagram Profile

Your Instagram professional profile should in no way resemble your personal Instagram account. And it is better that "you" rarely (if at all) appear on this Instagram page.

Here's how you can create a compelling Instagram profile that will help you improve your online presence to attract more customers:

biography screen instagram

A. Use an attractive bio

Experts also believe that an Instagram bio should prompt a customer to take action while highlighting the personality of the company.

Bio must be both interesting and informative. You should be able to hook your followers. You need to be convinced that adding Instagram users to Instagram will improve the content and value of your feed.

Provide details related to your business in a concise and relevant way. This should appeal to the Instagram community you are targeting and should also reflect the tone of your shared images. Also discover how to post multiple links in your Instagram bio.

B. Link to your site

Only Instagram bios can place clickable links, so please enjoy. A link to the site is shown in the space just below the description (at the top of the Instagram page).

Including links to websites is important to Instagram's marketing strategy. Make sure that the URL is readable, not a series of random characters. Also find a way to post multiple links to your Instagram bio.

Create an Instagram marketing strategy # 2: Build an Instagram aesthetic stream

Product images make a huge contribution to online shopping. Make Instagram your showcase to multiply this power.

Nearly 67% of all consumers rely on the product image before making their purchase decision and give them a higher priority than evaluations or product information.

Feel free to enhance your brand aesthetically while showing off your products.

biography screen instagram 2

A. Enhance your brand identity

You must be able to value the brand identity of your business. Most of the aesthetics of your Instagram feed will be based on the identity of your company. It's up to you to give the tone and the personality that you want to send back in the posted content.

B. Do not compromise. Focus on the target marke

Respond to your target audience without compromising on your brand identity. Please note that the Instagram feed is aimed primarily at current and potential customers. Find out what in your product or brand is most appealing to your target audience. And reflect that in the posted Instagram content.

C. Stay consistent

Your business will only gain brand identity if you remain recognizable. Make sure your Instagram profile image is consistent. Add the thumbnail of your profile picture to all your Instagram commitments and engagements

D. Find your competitors' strategies

Study the content of your competitors and get an idea of what they are promoting on Instagram and essential to get into your market. Do they use user-generated content for their products or services? What kind of content do they post to Instagram? How often ? What is their hashtag strategy ?

Get new information on what competitors are doing and new ways to improve your own marketing strategy.

Create an Instagram marketing strategy # 3: Be creative with your Instagram captions

Creative Instagram legends are one of the keys to attracting new customers, but it's not easy to find the right description for your image.

post jcrew instagram

A. Spend some time

Many users feel compelled to post images just after taking them. Instead of rushing, you need to take the time to properly define the caption of your image to captivate your audience. Your results will only be better.

B. Short but effective

Instead of unnecessarily stretching the legend, make it short but enjoyable. Remember, users will probably spend only a few seconds displaying your photo before moving on to the next one, make your text quality over quantity, through the description use your creativity to make the image more attractive. Do not be cold, but talk as you would outside the networks, it should boost your commitment. Instagram users hate formalities.

Create an Instagram Marketing Strategy # 4: Use Strategic Hashtags

Hashtags are used on Instagram to allow users to follow the content they are looking for. You should use hashtags strategically so that more users can find your posts during the search.

Here are some practices to help you get the most out of hashtags:

- Use less than 15 hashtags in each message.
- Select some frequently searched hashtags.

- Integrate hashtags that are only relevant to your target audience: reactions may be fewer, but more qualitative.
- In case of a brand specific hashtag, create hashtags that are branded.
- To make sure your brand in a local area, use location-based hashtags.

If you would like more information on the use and choice of your hashtags, click here.

Create an Instagram marketing strategy # 5: Create compelling stories on Instagram

Instagram has its most popular feature to be the Stories (400 million daily active users from June 2018). If you can relate stories to your brand identity, they will automatically connect you emotionally to your audience and add meaning to the content you post.

The stories you post contribute significantly to creating brand loyalty. Instagram offers you the best platform to post storieswhich gives credibility to the brand. But at the same time, your Instagram feed should reflect the purpose and image of your business (and your brand), as long as they create consistency. Random and disconnected content can be confusing. So be careful what you are about to publish.

Create an Instagram Marketing Strategy # 6: Develop a Committed Community

Since feeds on Instagram change quickly, it is likely that your content will be buried in no time. The only way to change this is to add hashtags to your posts on Instagram.

In fact, hashtags have an important role to play in placing your business in different communities on Instagram and are linked by a keyword, which will allow you to find your posts as long as Instagram is operational.

In addition, you can also consider inviting Instagram ambassadors to share your product / brand on their feeds. Creating a group of ambassadors to spread the benefits of your brand to their subscribers will help you reach and win more customers. Encouraging Instagram followers to post reviews and photos will also help you reach many other Instagram users.

Nearly 78% of all consumers buy products / services based on a brand's social media. As a result, the more people you have to share and promote your brand, the more likely you are to convince potential customers to buy your product.

Another great way to create an engaged community on Instagram is to share the marked photos of your subscribers on your Instagram profile, adding the content of your users to your own Instagram feeds will create a good feeling, which will then be associated with the brand you promote - 65% of Instagram users believe that when a brand talks about them, they feel happy and honored.

Get off the beaten path! Feel free to try new things. The Instagram algorithm changes constantly every half hour. So, everything that worked for you last week may not work for you the next week.

Therefore, it is best to continue experimenting with new ideas all the time. If they work well keep them, otherwise, try something new. Be original.

However, you can not avoid elements such as your brand content, high-quality images, user-generated content, engaging and engaging publications, and hot topics. The tips mentioned above will surely help you set up the best Instagram strategy.

HOW TO OPTIMIZE ACCOUNT AND SELL

How to optimize and sell an Instagram account?

If you already downloaded the application to your smartphone and got your Facebook account as registration data, or if you generated new credentials to access your new profile, stop here and see how to optimize please.

Basics about Instagram accounts

What everyone doesn't know when they decide to follow a sales strategy with a presence on Instagram is that this social network was originally designed to share images, and text has a place.

This doesn't mean it's impossible to implement a sales strategy on Instagram, but in that case you need to know tricks and practices to attract traffic that not everyone knows .

For example, to attract traffic to a website or a specific URL, you must do the following:

See the highlighted links you have in bios in your publication so that your followers can visit it.

Be sure to use the Instagram links correctly because you use dedicated

use #hashtags mostly to indicate your brands to increase visibility and reach more people.

Share a mini video introducing news on the website.

Unleash your imagination and share a clickable Instagram story that hooks the community from the start.

Instagram offers many possibilities for optimization and content creation in various formats, but you should be aware of the following restrictions:

Characters: The career limit is 29-150, but you can write a maximum of 2,200 for comments and text accompanying a post.

Tags: You cannot tag more than 20 people per post.

Hashtag: Up to 30 per post (never from a third party).

Follow-up: 200 follow and unfollow per hour.

Comments: 60 per hour.

Like: I like 100 other posts per hour.

Automation: Until very recently, this was not possible with external tools. Well, you may schedule publications from some of the most famous tools such as Hootsuite and SocialFlow in a somewhat less restrictive way.

Need some tips for Triunfagramers who want to sell on Instagram? Then write down:

Tag people you don't know or comment and like using an automated application! Please respect the restrictions that may cause you to lose your Instagram account labeled as a spammer.

Do not abuse the hashtag of each publication. Also, do not combine this practice with including additional comments.

Never forcibly get followers in a short time, like buying followers or following / unfollowing.

HOW DOES THE INSTAGRAM ALGORITHM WORK

There is no doubt that with the passage of time and especially from the relevance that Instagram took in this 2018, the publications do not have the scope that was previously available.

This is nothing new, it happened with Facebook several times. Precisely because of the changes in its algorithm.

Thus, it is important to know how the Instagram Algorithm works, in order to try to do things well and therefore increase the visibility of your account.

Currently the Instagram Algorithm is focused on certain key points, which we will see later:

- The engagement of your community.
- The interaction with your followers.
- The speed of interaction.
- The duration of the visualizations.
- The relevant hashtag.
- Do not act like a robot.
- Others.

Why is it important to know the Instagram Algorithm?

Knowing how the Instagram algorithm works has a direct impact on the visibility of your account.

This is simple, even if you do one or two things well, if

you want to grow your account or your competition has better results, it is probably due to this factor.

If you have a business account or want to improve your personal account, I always suggest analyzing the competition.

In short, you have to know your competition and know how to master the Instagram algorithm, in order to grow and increase your visibility in this social network.

The Instagram feed versus the Instagram timeline

Something I want to remind you before you start talking about the Instagram algorithm, is that you have to understand the difference between a feed and a timeline.

What is an Instagram feed?

The Instagram feed is the list of posts that appear within your account. Basically your publications in chronological order.

What is an Instagram timeline?

Instead the Instagram timeline, are the posts you see, when you enter the Instagram application.

You must learn to master the Instagram algorithm, in order to make your posts more visible on the timeline, beyond how beautiful, orderly or cool your feed is.

HOW TO BEAT THE INSTAGRAM ALGORITHM

Now, we are going to see recommendations based on the new Instagram algorithm , in order to overcome it and increase the visibility of your account.

1 - Increase engagement

The first thing you should know is that Instagram rewards publications that have a high dose of interaction (or engagement).

This means that Instagram takes into account the amount of likes, comments, views on videos, saved and others.

When you receive comments and I like in your posts that likes the algorithm of Instagram and therefore is a good sign for it

For example, a great way to increase engagement is that apart from uploading posts to your Instagram feed, take advantage of Instagram Stories since the algorithm also takes into account the interactions in them.

2 - Interact with your followers

It doesn't matter if you have a comment or hundreds of them, you should interact with the people who interact with your posts.

This is another factor that the Instagram algorithm

likes.

There is not much to say here. You have to worry about interacting and generating as many conversations as possible. That means that publication is being a success.

3 - The frequency of your posts

Instagram growth algorithm

Following the tips to master the Instagram algorithm , there is the issue of how often you make posts.

It's really about finding a balance.

Neither exaggerate making dozens of publications a day, nor spend days or weeks without publishing anything.

Look at it this way, the less time you spend updating your Instagram feed, you will have less interactions and therefore, your visibility will begin to decrease.

4 - The speed of interactions

This is somewhat complicated to achieve and has to do with affinity.

Imagine you have an accident, call 3 of your friends. One arrives in 5 minutes, another arrives in 6 hours and the other arrives in 3 days.

Which of your friends has more affinity with you?

Exactly, the first.

This is how affinity works on the Instagram algorithm. The faster the interactions of your followers with you, the better, because it means there is greater affinity.

How to achieve this?

Ideally, maintain a good relationship with your followers, interact often with them and most important of all, publish in the hours you know that most of your Instagram audience is connected.

5 - The duration of the visualizations.

Surely you did not imagine this, but the Instagram algorithm takes into account the time people spend viewing your post.

It's crazy not?

Obviously here you will have to use all your creativity to make people, while reviewing their Instagram timeline, stop to see your posts in detail.

So always think of having content that really makes people stop to look at it.

6 - Know your best times to post

My best schedules according to the Metricool planner

There is not much to say here.

If you want to increase your interaction rate, increase affinity and thus dominate the Instagram algorithm, you should know the best times to publish.

Some important questions you should ask are:

Who are my best followers?

Who interacts more with me?

What areas or countries are these people from?

What time are they most active?

What days of the week are they most active?

7 - The relevant hashtag

While the instagram algorithm penalizes excess hashtags (Shadowban), it also favors those publications that use relevant hashtags.

This means that before putting 15 or 20 hashtags to your posts, maybe with less than 5, but they are relevant, you can increase the visibility of your account.

So remember to analyze well what Instagram hashtags work best and don't forget not to overdo it, but above all, they are relevant.

TIP: Save different groups of hashtags relevant for different occasions in your smartphone's notebook. For example 4 or 5 hashtags for "dinners" or maybe for "party" or for "holidays"

8 - Post Instagram Stories or use IGTV

This is simple.

If Instagram brings out a new functionality, then you should take advantage of it because it surely affects the algorithm.

At the beginning Instagram was only for posting images. Then Instagram Stories joined and now there is Instagram TV (IGTV)

What does this mean?

What if you use Instagram Stories and also IGTV, you will surely like the algorithm and reward you with greater exposure.

9 -Don't act like a robot

Did you ever notice weird comments in your posts? Comments that simply have an emoji or a phrase like "good image" and nothing else?

It is very likely that they are Instagram bots.

Usually these Instagram bots are configured to follow certain accounts, follow certain hashtags and even comment with phrases that are predefined and are always short, with some emoji and may even be irrelevant to the publication.

Well, don't do the same.

For example, if all the comments of your followers, simply respond with a "Thank you" and a happy face, it is likely that over time the Instagram algorithm believes that you are a bot.

Be original, answer the comments, vary the phrases, generate conversation.

Don't be a meat and bone bot.

10 - Make Live Videos

Since 2017 Instagram allows you to make live videos, however, many of the accounts I follow do not usually use this feature.

If you want to grow on Instagram and beat the algorithm remember what I said before, you should take advantage of the functions of this social network.

Include in your Instagram strategy, publish live videos every so often.

Apart is a great way to interact with your followers.

11 - Take advantage of Trends

No, I do not mean that you join any challenge on the Internet, nor that you put aside your strategy to take advantage of a trend that has nothing to do with your account, brand or person.

But there are always trends that can be exploited.

Usually the trends are loaded with many topics of content, hashtags and even ways of communicating.

Take advantage of trends, are key to increase engagement and interactions at certain times.

12 - The use of Instagram features.

Finally, my last advice has to do with something I commented on several points.

If you want to master the Instagram algorithm, then it is key that you use all the functions that this social network has or leave.

It is simple, if Instagram launches a new functionality, it is very likely that its algorithm privileges those users who are early adopters, use them and even make them fashionable.

Before arriving late, my advice is to arrive early and take advantage of this new functionality, to boost your visibility.

MONETIZING YOUR INSTAGRAM PAGE

How to make money with Instagram: ways to monetize your account

1. Influencer marketing

Most users hate advertising and this is leading us to become more reluctant to direct and cold marketing actions.

It is clear that everyone who has a product or service needs to sell.

"Nobody likes to be sold, but everyone likes to buy!"

If you have a blog, you will know that the advertising banners make you lose credibility and that is why, in recent years, the influencer figure has become stronger and with greater conversion when it comes to promoting a certain product or service.

If you aspire to become an influencer thanks to Instagram , know that you don't need to be famous or have the measurements of a model.

What is now valued much more is the level of engagement , that is, the loyalty of the followers.

An example of this is Diana Miaus who has started collaborating with brands when she had only 20 thousand followers.

She, for example, is what dominates a micro-influencer , since it has a smaller community than others but at the same time very faithful to its contents.

At this point you could ask me: Serena, how can I become a micro-influencer?

Think about what you like, your passion, what you spend a lot of time.

Create a special relationship with your followers and do not become obsessed in the number of them, as in your level of engagement.

Simply put, interact with your followers to the fullest and build a solid and faithful relationship .

To do this, I recommend you also read these two articles:

13 most common mistakes you can't make on Instagram

How to use Instagram stories to grow your account

Once you have obtained a small community, you can register with these platforms to close your first collaborations:

- Tapinfluence
- Influenz
- The Mobile Media Lab
- SocialPubli
- Coobis
- Twync
- BrandBacker
- The shelf

You have to register and some of them not only ask for your Instagram account but also your blog and other social networks.

How to find collaborations on your own

There are many companies that still do not understand the potential of Instagram and why they should use this social network.

There are others who don't even have an account and don't even know what Instagram is.

So, what to do?

To avoid wasting time and not falling apart, I recommend that you focus on companies that already understand the potential of Instagram .

To do this, you can see what your "competition" does and see who they close collaborations with.

What I do is enter an account similar to mine, look at the post and see if there are particular mentions.

If the account in question has a blog, this information is usually found in «Contact», Media Kit or in the «Collaborations» section.

Once the first companies have been identified, I recommend you create a document where you can name them or better, create some notes on your mobile to remember them.

In this way, in a couple of weeks you can create your database with these potential accounts.

It will be much easier to start with companies with which they have already collaborated than to jump into the void.

2. Affiliate Marketing

If you have a blog, you'll know what I'm talking about.

If you do not have it, affiliate marketing means when you promote a product or service of another person and they pay you a percentage for each sale made.

On Instagram you can do it in two ways:

1. You can put the affiliate link in your BIO

2. Create a story , explain the product / service and add the link

There are many companies you can work with, such as:

Amazon Affiliates

Skyscanner

Airbnb

Tradedoubler

To shorten the link, customize it and track it, I recommend using bittly.com .

Also, if you want to better understand how this system works, I advise you to read this article by Frank de Lifestyle al Cuadrado : The mega guide of Affiliate Marketing.

3. Shout4shout

It is one of the methods that I have spoken to you in the Instagram guide and that many accounts use to grow quickly.

It consists of mentioning another account (for example in Instagram stories) and in turn, the other account does the same with yours.

This will make you known among his followers and the possibility of getting new followers in a very short time

If it is done with a great account, you will have many followers, likes and click on the link of your BIO.

There are also accounts that, to grow rapidly, are willing to pay for this type of collaboration.

In fact, if you have a page with millions of followers, you could charge about $ 40 - $ 200 for s4s (shout4shout).

Now think.

If you manage to sell a shou4shout a day, you could earn interesting money by spending a few minutes of your day.

Interesting right?

That's how young American Tim de @gentlemensmafia got rich .

His accounts have millions of followers and he created a network to exchange payment shout4shout.

But be careful, everything that glitters is not gold.

For a Shout4Shout to really work, you have to be careful:

to. Do not promote anything that is not typical of your niche

Do not forget that your followers follow you because they are interested in your page. If you propose something different, that does not fit with your niche, you could lose them.

b. Do not accept all kinds of offers

If the photo you are asked to promote does not convince you, do not do it.

4. Sell your photos

Although it is not as easy as it seems, there are people who earn money selling their photos.

As you can imagine, if you are a professional photographer, Instagram is the perfect showcase to publicize your works of art.

And these are some of the platforms where you can sell your photos:

Foap

Twenty20

5. Instagram as a source of traffic

People who ask me how to monetize their account always answer the same thing.

If you want to make real money with Instagram, the most common is that this social network is a source of traffic for your online business .

It is best to build a business that goes far beyond Instagram.

How?

For example, creating a blog or a web page , writing a guide or creating an email list.

If you get your followers to go to your sales page or your blog, you could get a lot of traffic.

Therefore, social media experts and marketers advise creating an Instagram page as a source of traffic for your blog and your e-commerce.

Instagram has great potential compared to other social networks such as Facebook.

Above all Instagram is free and if you want to invest money, ads are cheaper.

Then, engagement on Instagram is much higher than on Facebook .

Have you stopped to look at how many likes your last FB post has? And in IG?

6. Sell your Instagram account

If you have many accounts, you can create a true network.

And if one day you get tired of Instagram or want to leave this world, you can choose to sell your account, so that someone else uses it without having to start from scratch.

Where to sell it?

fame swap

viral accounts

CHAPTER FOUR

YOUTUBE MARKETING 2020

Over the years, YouTube became synonymous with opportunities to put your brand in evidence , because it is possible that you appear before your audience and that you have close relationships with content that stimulates interactivity.

Seeing that it is the most popular video platform in the world and the second most used search site on the planet, being present there is crucial for your company. On the other hand, YouTube is directly linked to Google, which can contribute to improve the positioning of your site in web searches.

Set up your study

If you want to make videos and spread them online, you need to have a good planning and invest in some particularities, such as the quality of your materials. Today, with so much content available on the internet, it is important to make investments so you can offer some quality.

Data behind the YouTube monster

- There are more than one billion users

- Every day hundreds of millions of hours are seen and billions of reproductions are generated
- 300 hours of video are uploaded every minute
- 50% of the reproductions are from mobiles
- Youtube is available in 75 countries and in 61 languages
- There are more than 1 million advertisers (most are small businesses

YouTube video marketing work is increasingly essential for a successful strategy. In the end, the contents of this type have a high potential to transmit information and contribute to the dissemination of products and services.

Although the content is the king on the web, it is very important that you worry about the most technical aspects, such as a study , which is one of the most appropriate solutions to help you save money with production and also have more dynamic processes and less bureaucratic

Then, before worrying about the equipment and all other things, the first step is to find a suitable place to set up the studio to record your videos, in order to meet your needs in terms of structure and equipment.

The space

Remember that the studio needs to have enough space for you to record your videos, for the equipment, the actors and the technical team. A place that is small can be very bad for the quality of the videos produced and also cause some kind of accident, since the production equipment is fragile and can be easily damaged.

Acoustics

Always look for places that are as distant as possible from noise. Always privileges the isolation of any type of sound that may hinder the recording.

Another recommendation to protect you from noise is through investments in expanded polystyrene plates or foams, which can be placed on windows and doors. On the other hand, egg maps are also efficient to make the acoustics of the environment better and you can place them above the foams.

Lighting and colors

If you were to use a closed room as a study, you should invest in lighting. Therefore, never forget that a poorly lit or shadowy scene can make your production ruined.

So, if you cannot count on natural light, which is very difficult, pay attention to illuminate the environment in the best possible way.

Another issue that needs attention is about the color of the environment you will use. In the end, depending on the paint and the color used on the wall, the light can be reflected with color and make your whole scene look bad.

Therefore, you should give preference to opaque paints, which absorb light instead of reflecting it. On the other hand, if you use a wall layer as the background of the images, choose the most neutral colors that do not cause much interference, in case they are reflected on products or people.

White ends up being an excellent option and, in case you want, you can always decorate the walls with paintings, clocks or elements that have to do with the content . If you have technical knowledge and want to produce more professional videos, it is worth investing in a chroma-key.

Finally, it is worth remembering that you must take care of the organization of the stage as a whole, that is, always have a beautiful and clean environment. This will bring a lot of credibility to the videos and will ensure you a number of subscribers on YouTube and, consequently, a participatory and connected audience.

Equipment Choice

The quality of videos is one of the essential factors for you to succeed in the YouTube strategy The good news is that there are investments for all budgets. You can record with a more solid camera and even with your smartphone.

It is important to invest in audio quality and good

lighting, which will make a leap in the quality of your recordings. Next, we will highlight some equipment for image, audio and lighting. Look!

Image

When opting for cameras, there are numerous models and prices. Regardless of whether you choose a smartphone, a webcam or a more compact camera, what is really worth is the budget. Then, study the possibilities:

tight budget : in case you have a cell phone with a good camera, preferably in Full HD, you will know that you have material that has advanced technology. A problem with the cell phone is the few focus adjustment options, but it is perfectly possible to record excellent videos for YouTube with the phone, duly attached to a tripod;

medium budget : the most compact cameras, depending on the model, are worse than many more recent cell phones. Because of that, it is very important that you pay attention and choose those that have a value similar to the input DSLR cameras;

Looser budget : DSLR cameras are the best bets for you to have optimal video quality. If you want something more practical, bet on that type of camera. But there are some simpler models within that category, such as the Canon T5 and Nikon D3200.

Audio

Audio is very important for recording quality videos. In the case of camera audio, it ends up being damaged by the environment, so the microphone ends up being necessary. In that case, pay attention to the possibilities:

tight budget : your smartphone probably has a microphone embedded in the hearing aid. It is not the most perfect scenario, but you can record your voice separately on the cell phone that way. Thus, you hide the hearing aid in the shirt and hold the microphone in the neck. The sound may not be so perfect, but it will probably be cleaner than the camera sound.

Medium budget : you have the option of investing in a lapel microphone with a connector that is serious in the smartphone. Recording with a lapel microphone, the sound quality of your video will be much better and your audio will be clear to your audience.

Looser budget: in case you record alone, invest in a lapel microphone and a digital recorder. You can find some kit options with good recorder microphones. Unquestionably, the result will be much better.

illumination

Good lighting is also essential to get your viewers to follow your videos from beginning to end. Although natural light works perfectly for different videos, you can also invest in some types of equipment, such as a panel of LED lights , which can be installed directly on the camera.

Although you can make more solid investments, as in the LimoStudio kit, which creates light and diffuse Illuminations, or in a Neewer Camera, a ring light, which is circular and can be installed in the camera.

Use YouTube video techniques in your favor

So that the work you present on YouTube has an excellent level of quality, you can use some filming techniques , which are essential to do a differentiated and successful work. Below, we highlight recommendations that may be indispensable for your strategy. Let's go to them:

- lighting: a well-lit video is vital for your content to be viewed in a completely comfortable way by the viewers, since it prevents data, information and some places from being hidden;
- animations: animations offer endless possibilities for you to create your videos. They give dynamism to your content and can be another attraction for people to really be attentive to your ideas;
- narration: some more complex concepts can become a very difficult task to express. Therefore, a more personal narrative can make all the difference when explaining some ideas;
- music: choosing a music that transmits the

desired emotions is an excellent way to give strength to the contents of the videos ;
- humor: using humor is another way of fixing the public's attention in a general way, but you must do that in a very timely manner and avoid excessive informality;
- graphics: listing the fruits on the performance of a company in the course of the video can become somewhat boring, but through the use of infographics it is possible to make the understanding of information easier, in addition to avoiding reading the numbers;
- emotion: telling exciting stories are great ways to pass the company's message to the public and can make the connection with customers established. On the other hand, it is worth remembering that exciting videos sell more;
- Duration: choosing how long a video will last is a very important technique, since it is essential to find a balance between the speed in which ideas are expressed and the period in which the user will be attentive to the video;
- colors and filters: using colors and image filters is essential to give more depth to the messages and these can be used both in more comparative videos, as in others with more educational character;

Company history: telling a brief history of the company and its processes so far is an essential technique to value all the progress achieved. On the other hand, it reinforces the identity and image of the brand.

Success in the type of content

Ensure you use content that is really relevant to your audience . The contents must really solve the problems of your audience and to help you in this task we will highlight 10 content ideas for YouTube. Look!

1. Explanatory videos

People really like video tutorials, in which things are explained in detail . Making videos that clarify people's doubts is a great way to have many views and participation.

2. Promotional videos

It is necessary to pay attention to the promotions of products and services that your audience has interest. Based on this, you can create content for some promotions you are doing . Remember that everyone likes a promotion and you can exploit that strategy in a timely manner.

3. Vlogs

People love to know details of the racks in people's lives. Therefore, if it were something that suits your business, you can make more informal videos, telling about content you learned, events you participated, among other issues .

4. Recommendations

People like to receive recommendations of all types. Therefore, if you have any ideas or are experts in some subjects, make videos indicating ideas that will certainly help your audience.

5. Make webinars

Webinars are live videos in which you can give a class or a dissertation. Its duration usually varies and depends a lot on the subject and the type of audience you want to reach. It is an excellent way to establish closer relationships with potential consumers and create your authority in the market.

Audio Marketing: the evolution of content

Undoubtedly, audio is the type of multimedia that can best adapt to the routine: even with the existence of other content distribution formats, it lost its importance.

Read more "

6. Product Reviews

The product review is one of the video ideas that generate the most views. Nowadays, many people go to the internet to know details of a product and that can be an excellent idea to spread your merchandise and promote your brand.

7. Customer stories

You can promote some videos by telling success stories of some clients. Remember that people connect more easily with other people than with brands.

8. Videos on how to do

Many people go to the internet to solve their problems. From the moment you create videos teaching people to do things, you will naturally build a good audience.

9. Personal videos

People like to know about experiences. Therefore, if you have any interesting personal history that refers to the professional context, you can exploit that in the videos and generate very identification with your audience.

10. Motivational videos

Motivational videos are also an excellent idea for you to identify with your audience and make him participate with your brand.

Configure the YouTube channel

In case you have finished creating a YouTube channel, we will give you essential recommendations for you to stand out. Follow, below, some channel configuration recommendations:

1. Add channel art and profile picture

It is very important that you add an art for the channel and a profile picture to have a visual identity that is easily recognized by your audience. For the profile (or avatar), it is interesting that you have a logo and for the art (or cover photo) you can use images that establish a synergy of your work with what you will address in your channel.

2. Add a description and the client of your other digital platforms

To describe your business, it is interesting to tell a little about your story and your proposal on YouTube . It is worth presenting, for example, your mission, vision and values. It is also an excellent opportunity to add links from other platforms, such as Facebook, Instagram and Twitter. For that, you need to go to the settings and enable the option "Customize the layout of your channel".

3. Upload videos

To upload a video on YouTube, you just need to click on the arrow icon, which is at the top edge, to the right of the screen . Next, the tab will appear to upload the video. You have the option to select several videos or, if not, you can upload one at a time.

An important recommendation is that, at the time of uploading, you should place the videos in the private option. That way, you can edit it before it is released to the public. After having everything correct, you can put the video as public.

4. Understand the differences between public, unlisted and private

On YouTube, there is a possibility that you configure the privacy of videos. There are three options and each of them has some peculiarities:

Private: When you select this option, videos cannot be viewed by the channel owner. It is recommended to place it in private when the video is not yet finished or when you wish that no one else has access to its content;

Not listed: through this option, your video can only be seen by the people you want, that is, the general public will not be able to access. In that case, the channel owner sends the video link to the people he wants to see.

Public: This option allows the video to be open on your channel and viewed by anyone who searches.

Create a check-list

To be successful with your YouTube video strategy, it is very interesting that you have a check-list to highlight all the steps of your videos. In the first moment, you can check your steps in four situations:

1. Preproduction

At this stage, you need to be aware of issues such as duration, format, quantity of videos and content management . Here, it is also the ideal time for you to write a video script, fully aligned with the needs and motivations of your audience.

2. Production

After deciding what will be done and produced, the ideal is to implement the content strategy defined in the previous item. Some content corrections will also be made, because many times what was put on paper is not very good in the video . On the other hand, in this stage the care related to the place of the recording, the formats and the angles also correspond so that everything goes perfectly.

3. Post production

After recording a video according to the planning of the previous stages, it is necessary to learn how to edit videos , in order to correct the possible imperfections that are in the content. At this stage, the entire video must be evaluated before being released by means of opinion tests between the teams and the management of the company .

4. Disclosure

This is one of the most important stages for professionals involved in the video marketing strategy for YouTube. After all, remember that, with good content in hand, the possibilities of a video are unlimited .

In this case, it is worth the disclosure on the site itself in social networks in e-mail marketing, so that you guarantee the effective opening rate and, mainly, a greater conversion in relation to other types of format.

In addition to evaluating each of these stages, it is essential that you are attentive to the SEO strategy for YouTube , so that your video can appear well positioned on Google . To stand out, it is necessary to invest in the following techniques:

- always use keywords in the title;
- know all the tools of Youtube and learn how to exploit them;
- effectively describe your video and learn to use tags;
- share it on social networks, sites and wherever you can;
- use calls for action (CTAs) in videos.

STEPS TO CREATE YOUR YOUTUBE CHANNEL

But I don't roll up anymore and let's get to the important thing. I will explain how to create your own YouTube channel in just 5 steps ! And if you don't believe me ... you just have to keep reading.

We start!

Step 1: Sign in with your Google account

Firstly, log in with your Google account. This step is essential, because without logging into Google you will not be able to create it.

Step 2: Go to the YouTube page

For now you cannot tell me that this is being complicated, since you have only had to do a few clicks! And if you think that the thing is going to start getting complicated, you are wrong, because creating your YouTube channel is going to be eating and singing. I assure.

The next thing you have to do is visit the YouTube page . Once there, at the top right you will find your icon or photo, depending on the data you have completed in your Google account.

Click on it and choose the option «My channel» . If even with the explanation you are still a little confused, look at the image below, in it I show you where to click. So don't panic!

Step 3: Choose the name of your channel

This is where the interesting begins, and the really important thing for your YouTube channel . It is at this moment, when doubts assail you and when suddenly a thousand questions come to your head.

Think about the name of your YouTube channel when you create it!

For all that and because I am very nice, I have added a section where I give you my best advice when choosing a name for your channel.

How to choose the name of your YouTube channel?

The name of your channel is very important and before launching to put any one I recommend that you think carefully. Do not forget that it will be the first thing users see and it will be directly related to the searches they do. There is nothing!

So remember:

The name must be related to the theme of the channel or the name of your brand.

Use shorter names

Do not use symbols, signs, dashes or numbers.

If you don't have a lot of imagination or you can't think of any name for your channel, I recommend you use tools that help you generate names, such as Business Name Generator.

At the end of the whole, when you are filling in the different fields on the YouTube page, you will see the option Use a company name or another name?. I want to explain the difference:

With a personal account you can only have a single YouTube channel associated with your account.

If you use a brand channel , you can have multiple channels associated with your account. These channels are also known as brand accounts. You can also add additional administrators and owners to your brand account and manage your channel together with your collaborators or teammates without the need to share passwords.

I would recommend this last option . But you have the last word.

Step 4: Customize your channel

Here you must customize your channel . That is, you must associate it with your brand image. To do this, use the colors and corporate images of your company or business.

Keep in mind that the design of your channel is essential to make a

good first impression to your followers , so do not skimp on time.

Your followers, know them well!

And above all, take care of the details , this will make your YouTube channel make a difference with respect to others of similar content, or with respect to your competition.

Advice, complete all the required information, be original and above all make use of quality images.

Completing the channel information and using good quality images will not only help you gain followers. If not, which also will help your channel to like the YouTube algorithm more . That is, all advantages!

So, so that you are not lazy or lazy, I leave you a small guide where you can and complete the information with quality!

Channel Icon

Channel Icon will be your sign of identity . Therefore, you must choose a quality image and according to the channel you are creating.

For example, if it is a company, the right thing is to use your company logo . If it is a personal channel, I recommend the logo of your personal brand, or a photo that is associated with you.

Channel header or banner

The header is the largest image of your entire channel , so think well that you will show on it.

Choose a perfect cover that reflects your spirit or that of your brand. When designing it, you must take into account the different formats depending on the devices from which it will be displayed (smartphone, tablet, desktop computer, etc.).

Therefore you must ensure that the most relevant is seen from all devices, that is, that it is located in what is known as a safe area. And how can you know? Well, very simple:

When you upload the image, in the preview pop-up, you will see how it looks on each of the devices.

These are the sizes you should use:

YouTube channel icon 800 × 800

Header size for YouTube channel 2580 × 423

How can you create covers for your YouTube channel?

You may not have knowledge or resources to make the header of your YouTube channel. For this reason, I leave here some tools with which you can create original, creative and professional covers.

Best of all, is that with these tools you can also create your own header for your channel in a very fast and simple way.

Canva

Desygner

Crello

If in this process you also need to use royalty - free images with high resolution. I recommend you visit these pages:

Pixabay

Pexels

Unsplash

Complete your channel information

Now, what you have left to do is complete basic aspects of your channel. To do this, I leave some tips:

Make a brief description of your channel . It is a huge necessity to tell the public what they are going to see in your videos.

The location .

You can add an email address so they can contact you if your channel is commercial.

You must also add links to your website or different profiles on social networks.

The above is essential to attract the attention of the public and end up visiting the content of your channel.

You see the difference? Which of the two do you find most attractive ? The answer is more than obvious!

Step 5: Upload your first video

To do this you can click on the link "Upload a video" . You just have to start uploading the file and choose your privacy: public, hidden, private or scheduled.

But what is the difference between hidden and private?

Well, the truth is that these two concepts are very easy to understand. In fact, here I leave the distinction between the two:

Hidden : Hidden videos can only be viewed by those users who have the video link.

Private : A private video can only be seen by the user who uploads it and by the people he chooses.

STEPS TO MONETIZE YOUTUBE VIDEOS

There are several steps we can take to monetize YouTube videos but first of all, you must have your own YouTube channel, that you have generated content of interest and above all that you see that your subscribers are growing. As soon as you see that, you can start on how to monetize the videos you upload with these steps:

AdSense and YouTube

It is probably the best known method also because it is in front of everyone's eyes. Do you know those ads that are seen before and after YouTube videos?

Well, this means that the channel you're visiting adheres to the YouTube partner program and monetizes the channel with AdSense.

What is it?

In practice, every time someone shows an ad, there is a small benefit. The monetization system is based on the CMP, that is, the cost per thousand. That is, the advertiser (who is the one who invests in advertising) pays a total for every thousand people who see your ad.

Youtube in turn divides the income with the youtuber but do not believe that the amount you will earn at the beginning is going to be a lot. It is said that the average in Spain with the program of partners and with the ads is about three euros, but the reality is different and there are many videobloggers who claim to charge just a few cents for each video with integrated ads.

This is due to the many changes that YouTube has made within its partner program in recent years and months specifically. In fact, it was recently announced that YouTube has introduced a new limitation for smaller channels. Thus, from now on, to join the partner and Adsense program, you must have more than 1,000 members and a total of 4,000 hours of "observation time" accumulated during the year. So write this down to start thinking about being from the program, let the ads begin and you can charge for it, no matter how small.

Affiliations

Affiliations are another method used by a YouTuber to make money with YouTube. But what exactly are they? It's very simple: it's about recommending products (or services) and taking a commission every time someone buys that product through the link we put for them to buy.

But as in the previous section, commissions are variable, although it is said that with this second method, the percentage can be up to even 70%, but of course to reach that level you must be a YouTuber with millions of followers and as No, of visualizations.

Influence marketing

Similarly to the previous point, there is also influence marketing. That is, you appear in a video drinking a certain brand drink or wearing the clothes of a particular firm. That is to say, to indirectly advertise in your videos, of brands that pay you for it.

Sell own products and services

Here a real world opens up. For what reason? Because the possibilities become virtually endless. Depending on our type of channel, we can offer connected services or create ad hoc products.

It is nothing new for a YouTuber with a certain popularity or fame, to end up publishing a book, take out his line of clothes, make-up or also launch a new product. Without a doubt, if you have millions of followers, it will allow you to earn a lot of money, but it is still an expansion of "business" to which only those who already have a certain weight in the YouTube world aspire at the moment.

On YouTube there is a world of users who have created an empire behind their channel, so with the points indicated, you know what steps to take to achieve them all and realize your dream of making money with YouTube.

types of ads that exist on YouTube .

TRICKS TO IMPROVE YOUR YOUTUBE CHANNEL

YouTube is not only a video platform but it is also the second most important social network of the present and safe of the future. Any company that wants to promote itself in networks is essential to create and promote your YouTube channel in order to increase your visits and generate a better return on investment for your business company or personal brand.

1. Optimize your content on your YouTube channel to have a good SEO

YouTube is not just uploading a video and that's it. You need to do an SEO process to make your channel visible.

The YouTube algorithm takes into account many factors to make your channel more visible against competing videos. To do this you need, first of all, to choose the basic keywords that you will have to implement in order to be able to implement them in the names of the video files that you upload, in the titles, descriptions, tags, annotations, playlists with keywords, etc.

2. Create very good titles for your video

Something very important is to create a good title for your video , and not precisely chosen at random, but by doing a keyword research with free tools such as google keyword planner or KWFinder or with payment tools such as Sistrix or Semrush

The title of your video on YouTube should call the action and also be an informative title.

Click To Tweet

Your title should not be extensive but direct with what you have in that video. I give you an example so you can understand it better.

Checkout an optimized title and another not so well optimized:

Optimized: 3 Actions to improve the CONVERSION of a digital business, with Ricardo Tayar.

Not Optimized: Conversion actions of a digital business.

In the first case, I not only made a call to action listing the actions that will be counted in the video but also capitalized the word that I consider key in the video and also named the author of this video .

In the case of the not optimized, it can be seen that it is a much more generic title, that does not attract attention like the other and does not invite you to click on it to visualize it.

3. Create clear and attractive YouTube thumbnails

Although YouTube gives you to choose 3 thumbnails to choose from the video, they may never reflect what you want to capture with them and you will not get interaction with them. The thumbnails are a fundamental part to get the click and I will tell you the steps to follow to be able to have some great custom miniatures.

Create mini-hooks that hook and make the viewer interested in your content.

Click To Tweet

The importance of Clickbait on YouTube

Clickbait is that "cyberanzuelo" that makes your thumbnail image attractive to the user and click with your mouse on your video. There are good and bad clickbait. The bad thing is that the thumbnail does not correspond to the content of the video but it does make you enter it, but later ... when you see that its content is not what it promised, you will leave this video. The opposite is the good one, that the thumbnail not only corresponds to the video but also to the title of the video, everything has a coherence and makes you finally watch that video.

Think that the thumbnail will look a fairly small size, even less if viewed from a mobile device therefore, do not use many letters and less in an illegible size since they will not be visible and people will not click on your video. It should also reflect the content of this video.

miniaura youtube

Tips for creating thumbnails: The close-ups of the face work very well, large texts with brightly colored backgrounds, contours in letters or silhouettes making the image more dynamic.

YouTube mini-books must have a resolution of 1280 × 720

Click To Tweet

Make sure you upload your thumbnails with a maximum size of 2MB and in .JPG format

4. Fill in the keywords of your channel very well, verify your account and complete all your data in your profile

Make your channel like a home. That is, that people enter your channel and everything is well structured, with everything well optimized, your profile picture is optimal, your background is well trimmed so that it looks correct on all devices and generates a good description and trailer in your channel.

The description of your channel is the cover letter, the first thing a user sees when entering your channel, do not miss this opportunity and start well from the beginning.

Include links to your social networks

youtube cover

It is very possible that people who watch your videos are interested in getting into your social networks. Make it easier by indicating all these social networks. I tell you in a little trick so that the name of your entire website appears as it appears in the photograph above.

It is possible that in the new version of YouTube does not let you change the links or enter them from scratch, therefore go to the old version from the top right on your profile and select the last option that is to go to the previous version of YouTube. From there follow these steps:

youtube channel

Click on the cogwheel and check that you have active the option "customize the design of your channel"

Thanks to this enabled option you will be able to visualize the option of links that will be shown where you previously changed the background image on your channel, that is, on the top right, click on the pen and click on «edit links. There you will arrive right at this screenshot

YouTube profile

As you will see in the first option it is the only one that will appear all the text, so instead of putting «web» put your web directly without the http: // as it appears in the image and so you can show your web in a way Visual much better.

5. Do not disconnect and stay active in your channel constantly

Not only worth uploading a video and waiting for likes and comments. Those likes and comments will come up when you generate that necessary interaction with your audience. Respond to comments on your videos and comment on other people's videos that are references to you. With this you will make your audience much more committed to you.

Have people subscribe to your channel and do not forget that "hit the bell" that is, not only activate the subscription to your channel but also activate the alert for when you upload a new video. This notice is located right next to the subscription button.

The constancy on YouTube is a fundamental factor to grow your audience.

6. Use the Lead Magnet technique on your YouTube channel

There are different ways to capture customers in your channel but one of the best is through Lead Magnet or subscriber acquisition giving something in return. It consists of giving something valuable to your users in exchange for their email or subscription, such as Luis Villanueva , Neil Patel , Vilma Núñez or Javier Elices use this strategy and it works great. Of course, the content you offer has to be of value and oriented to your audience.

What can you offer in your Lead magnet strategy?

You can offer ebooks, a pdf guide of the video content so that they also have it in written format, templates to help the client in different billing services, design, events etc ...

To do this you must generate calls to action (CTA) of different types such as creating an entradilla and an end in your videos that encourage you to download the gift in the description of the video itself or also generating a card on YouTube inviting people to subscribe

Insert a link from your Lead Magnet at the beginning of your video description

Once you've generated this Lead Magnet, don't just put it on your YouTube channel. Move your video through social networks such as Facebook, Twitter, Instagram or Linkedin and you will see how constancy will start your followers to grow.

7. Use Adwords as a tool to generate audience

You can make your video come out related to other videos through the Google Adwords Discovery option , with this advertising you will allow the user to click on your video. The other option is called trueview , it is the option in which your video will be launched at the beginning of the visualization and that the user will be able to spend 5 seconds even 30 seconds. That is, if the client clicks to exit the video before those 30 seconds it will not count as a visualization.

This advertising is great to generate Branding for your brand, you may not convert if you sell a product but what you will do and at a very economical price is to generate that visualization of your service, product or personal brand among others.

8. Generate a post of your own video

A very good option is to be able to generate a post by transcribing your video and giving valuable content on your blog. With this you can give a new written and valuable content, complementing your video with valuable content. Not only can you do it in this order but you can also generate a video from a post you made earlier. Take advantage of this opportunity and create new keywords positioned in your blog and increase the time spent by inserting the linked video in your post.

inserting a video in your blog you will gain time of permanence.

Click To Tweet

9. Generate playlists

By generating playlists on your channel you can make your users consume one video after another. Not only will you be able to insert videos from your channel into this list, but also related videos from other channels and influencers, creating variety in your lists and making it possible for anyone interested in similar videos from your industry partners to reach yours as well.

With the playlists you can also position your videos because by generating these lists you enrich the keywords and help the YouTube search engine to position your content.

10. Use final screens and cards in your videos

Use final screens

they will appear in the last 20 seconds of your video and keep in mind that to insert final screens, your video must have at least 25 seconds. The final screens will encourage new subscriptions and also new views to other videos.

YouTube gives importance to generate these final

screens, therefore take this opportunity and think before generating the video, that is, in the edition, and leave those seconds later to be able to generate your final screen in the video.

Imagine that you forget to leave those final 20 seconds in your video and you are explaining with a Screencast something important and just two videos are placed as final screens and make the content of your video is not visible. Therefore it is essential to think about that time and in the edition place a previously created screen for these final screens, here I show you an example:

Final score   Final Screen

Reserve in the edition of your video the last 20 seconds to insert your final screens

Use cards in your video

With this option you will create links to other videos or playlists, you can promote your channel, do surveys and also link your website. These options, both the final screen and the cards are visible from mobile and are configured in the edition of each video. I leave a screenshot where you can see exactly where these menus are located for configuration.

11. Partner with other youtubers

If you want to grow on a YouTube channel is to be able to partner with other youtubers , but you may wonder

... how can I approach them? You will have to be especially original, and why not ... Generate a video and address that person privately, offer your services, your tutorials or simply thank the work you are doing, create a link with this person or company and you will make it possible for He also looks at you and if he likes what you do he can help you in different ways. .

If this option comes out it can be a great strategy to increase your reach and create new subscribers.

12. Use original and royalty-free songs

A fundamental error when starting a YouTube channel is to insert in your videos, known songs protected by copyright, this is not a correct action since you not only run the risk of your video being blocked, but even if it is not blocked, rest assured that you won't be able to monetize it.

You never know if a video of you can grow on visualizations or be sponsored, therefore, my advice is to always use royalty-free songs. You have many pages that allow you to have these options, even YouTube itself allows you to choose from thousands of songs prepared to monetize your videos and of course, royalty-free. You can find it in your menu at the bottom left in the "CREATE" section.

13. Use YouTube analytics

Analyze the content of your channel, see the visits you receive, where they come from, how old are your followers and an endless number of tools that YouTube offers for free within your channel, specifically on the left side "analytics" you can see the viewing time of each video, and something very important, the retention of the audience. Fundamental parameters to know what video works and learn from your audience to improve your statistics.

CHAPTER FIVE

TWITTER MARKETING 2020

Twitter has over three hundred million active users monthly and a young user base that boots, Twitter is a great platform for most marketers.

Setting up a company Twitter page is quick and easy to setup. All you need is to upload a profile picture, fill out a bio, and send the first tweet. However, not so simple is to expand your Twitter account, turn it into a real tool, get leads and build your brand.

To increase the number of real followers on Twitter, it's not enough to send a tweet whenever a company releases a product or holds an upcoming event. Interact with your target audience and interact with them. Successful Twitter marketing is powerful. If you become a professional on this fast-paced social networking site, you will gain new opportunities to grow your business online.

Twitter differences

The approach to all social media sites must be different. For example, Twitter's marketing strategy is different from Pinterest and Facebook's marketing plans. Understanding how Twitter works and where it fits in the social media environment determines how you use Twitter.

The main ways companies use Twitter are:

- Sharing information and content
- Promote engagement in promotional activities
- Interaction with consumers
- networking
- Increase brand visibility

All these are related to interactions. For example, it's not just broadcasting content like Instagram and Pinterest. Twitter makes communication successful. Keep this in mind as you continue the rest of this guide and delve into the heart of Twitter marketing.

Beyond the tips on "Setting up your profile correctly" and "Following influencers". Learn about the actual Twitter marketing strategy to be more successful and the steps necessary to do professional marketing. If you are interested in how to market your business on Twitter, keep reading.

Twitter chat: Undeveloped market

For years, marketers have asked the question "How can I increase my Twitter followers?" The question I really want to ask is "How can I increase my active Twitter followers?" The answer is Twitter chat. I have been promoting Twitter chat for quite some time. It's great to see a lot of marketers gradually starting to recognize the power of Twitter chat when it comes to getting positive followers.

The reason why Twitter chat is so effective is that people who participate in Twitter chat enjoy active participation in social networks. It is not just used for content distribution and consumption. Instead, these people use Twitter for the intended purpose, that is, to interact. These are the types of users who respond to tweets, retweet content, or expand messages.

To get started, look for industry-related Twitter chat. Whether you are in the marketing industry or are targeting business owners and entrepreneurs, Chloe West has compiled a great resource for the latest Twitter chat on topics such as content marketing, social media, and business. You can also use Google at any time.

Can't find an industry Twitter chat? Let's start by yourself. The key to success in Twitter chat is to be more than an audience. You need to add value to the conversation and differentiate it. Using tools such as Canva, you can create beautiful Twitter images very easily within minutes.

Canva social media image size

Another tip to gaining loyal followers during Twitter chat is to reply to other chatters. Most of the tweets must be in reply to others. Don't forget to @mention to receive notifications. Finally, follow up on the new connection you created during the chat.

Create a Twitter list for each participating Twitter chat and add the participating users to the list. Then start retweeting, posting to favorites, replying to tweets, and sharing content. Make sure that the relationship does not disappear after the Twitter chat ends.

HOW TO LEVERAGE TWITTER AS A MARKETING TOOL

How to use twitter as an Online Marketing tool?

Twitter online marketing Twitter is one of the best known and most important social networks after Facebook. So what we have to ask ourselves is: How to take advantage and use twitter in our favor is to say, to loyalty, profitability our business or company? . Twitter has surprised the world with its exponential growth and its ability to keep millions of people connected tweeting 24 hours a day, every day of the week and throughout the year.

It has a worldwide reach , you can follow favorite people, friends, mentors, etc. wherever they go and know what they are doing almost in real time. You can also use Twitter to increase your sales, get customers, branding your company as a professional.

Using Twitter as an online marketing tool will help you expand your business or company. The nature of

Twitter is perfect for promoting your business due to the speed with which you can literally deliver your message to millions of people and around the world.

To launch an online marketing campaign and virally you only need a laptop and / or a PC with an Internet connection, it is no longer necessary to have a laptop but you can do it from your smartphone or iPhone . As you will see, marketing and the way of communication has changed radically in recent times.

Knowing how and why viral marketing works will help you understand when you use Twitter. In a nutshell, the theory is that you send a message (tweet) to your friends list about something you are doing at the time. The process is that they will send a Retuit "RT" to their lists or to their contacts and so on until thousands of people see your message. There are hundreds if not millions of people to respond to any call to action you have proposed in your message, such as "Find out here", "Enter Now", "Click", etc . There are good chances that some of those people were called to buy your service or product, all thanks to this Twitter Social Network.

When using Twitter as an Internet marketing tool or online marketing , you have to keep in mind that, due to its nature, your messages must be updated and frequently. With each message that is sent, the effectiveness of viral marketing tends to decline, so YOUR CONTENT must be INTERESTING and HIGH IMPACT to keep people's attention. Beyond this, it is one of the most effective ways to Do internet marketing.

Do you need to promote your product or service? Twitter is one of the most suitable tools for this. It is proven that Twitter is growing very fast and is giving a lot to talk around the world and everywhere. This works very well, but as in everything it is essential that you know how to use it correctly to be successful when marketing for your business or company.

MARKETING ON TWITTER IN 2020

Basics to better understand Twitter

What would a definitive guide be without the basics! Here is a short glossary so you can better understand this post and go hand in hand. ☺

Hashtag: Word that can be directly searched for your results by clicking. Usually, they are popular words or short phrases. They use the # symbol.

Lists It is a group of selected accounts that groups their content.

Mentions Way in which another user is called by tagging it. It is also considered a mention in response to some other person's tweet.

Direct message: Private messages that you can send to another person.

I like it. Heart shaped button to the right of a tweet. It serves to assess the content of the profile.

Retweet: Tweet from another profile that you forward to your followers.

Follower: Account that follow your profile to receive your tweets on your timeline.

Following: They are the people that you follow from your profile and you can see their tweets in your chronology.

Timeline Chronology of the tweets that generate the profiles you follow in real time.

Trending: Topic Popular themes or hashtags at the time of consultation

Tweet: It is an element composed of text, images, GIFs, videos or URLs.

BENEFITS OF USING TWITTER FOR YOUR COMPANY

There are many benefits that small, medium and large companies obtain when using Twitter. The main one is that it creates a direct and fast communication channel between your company and your current clients.

I share some of the benefits of Twitter for any company:

Benefit from trends. Twitter lets you know what the

relevant topics your audience is talking about. It will allow you to participate in a useful way among your followers. For example, if you have a hotel and you see that in the trends there is a hashtag like #HoyPuedo, write a tweet where you include the trend: "#Today I can relax in the pool" and add a photo of the hotel pool.

Offer customer service. According to Twitter, for 85% of followers of small businesses on Twitter, it is relevant that they offer customer service from this social network. Following the example of the hotel, through Twitter you can promote discounts or packages, respond to comments and doubts that are generated or even generate reservations.

Create relationships with potential customers. Start or participate in conversations that are of interest to your company and create connections that may be something else in the future. Returning to the example, if you find conversations with related topics such as vacations, hotels or rest, you can interact in that conversation by inviting them to your hotel.

Increase the reach of your brand. Use your company's profile to increase the reach of your brand. If you have already optimized the profile with hotel data, location, telephone and logo, start interacting with profiles outside your community.

COMMON MISTAKES THAT ARE MADE ON TWITTER

The most common mistake in any social network is when you do not finish editing your profile.. There are many reasons: because it is lazy to finish it, because they want to go straight to tweet or just because it is a requirement of something without needing to use it. If you don't add your logo as a profile picture, nobody will know you. If you don't add a biography, they won't know what your company is about.

Follow and not interact. It will be inappropriate to use your Twitter account to tweet and follow people only without interacting with them. Remember, quality is better than quantity, followers who interact with you and share your content.

Get followers desperately. Or better known as the #followback and demand that they follow you. It is also a common mistake to buy followers, they will not add value to your profile and would denote distrust of observing a massive number of followers but that there is no mutual interaction.

Steal other people's content. Give a bad impression of your brand and image, as well as distrust. Take a moment to create your content according to the strategy you chose.

Fight. It doesn't matter if they are attacking your brand

or someone made a claim response for your product or service. Provide kind answers and give a solution to your problem.

Use your account as spam. You can promote your brand but so that Twitter does not consider your spam account - or users report to you -, share only 20% of your posts a day for the promotion of your brand.

Before you start, create your profile

Have you heard the saying "the first impression is never forgotten"? Well, on Twitter for companies the profile is the first impression of your company or personal brand and yes, it is important and counts. I will show you the elements of a profile on Twitter and how to configure them to professionally show your company or brand.

Know the elements of a profile

To create your profile effectively, you must understand what elements make up a profile to tailor yours and generate a good impression.

Your user name. It is what users will identify you on Twitter. It can consist of up to 15 characters and goes after an arroba. The name you choose is with which users can search for you and mention you.

Profile picture. The photo is small, 400 x 400 px. Remember to choose an image that represents your company or brand as the logo. This image, besides being always visible on your profile, will be in every tweet you publish.

Biography. This is a brief description of you or the company as to why they should follow you. Always include basic information about your company such as location, hours or contact forms. In addition, it offers you the option of adding a link to your website.

Header Image Or also cover image, serves to highlight something you want to highlight the company visually. The image must have a size of 1500 x 500 px and can be a PNG image or a JPG.

Tweet set. It is a tweet that stays at the top of your timeline in your profile. It serves to highlight a tweet with important information and when people enter your profile do not miss it.

Once you understood the elements, start creating your profile.

What to tweet?

Hands to the keyboard! The time has come to tweet.

The time has come to tweet

There is no specific rule for tweeting. You are free to write - only 280 characters stop you - and add the content you want in a single tweet. Nor is there a limit of tweets per day.

I can only give you some tips so that you get the interest of your audience when you tweet.

Write short tweets. Use a tweet for each message you want to convey. Be brief and specific.

Use visual content. You can add images, videos, GIFs and even live streams in a tweet. This type of content always generates interaction. You can include up to 4 images in a tweet.

Use the hashtags. They allow you to expand the reach of your tweet. Use hashtags that are relevant to your company or personal brand. I recommend using between 1 and 3 tags per tweet.

Make questions. Through the tool to create surveys -or with open questions in text-, you can launch questions of interest among your followers, that interact and even create conversations in the answers.

Answer Retweets. You can retweet some content of interest to your audience or your company or personal brand and write something when sharing it. In addition to generating content in your timeline, you can network with a retweeted user.

Interact The city of Rome was not forged in a day and neither will your community. The interaction will work as a tool to create loyalty between your followers and you, as well as an interest in your profile because you have shown interest in theirs!

Use of Twitter Lists for companies

A Twitter List is a group of accounts that you select in order to have a timeline with only the content of those accounts. The Lists can be created from your account or subscribe to Public Lists of other users. In case you create your own list, you decide whether to make it public or private.

The Lists will help you segment the people you follow a little more in detail and you can interact with them better.

HOW TO CREATE YOUR LIST ON TWITTER

1. Click on the "profile and configuration" button.

Step 1. Profile and configuration2. From the drop-down list, select Lists.

Step 2. Select Lists

3. Create a list on the "Create new list" button on the right side.

Step 3. Create new list

4. Add a name to the list and if you wish, a short description.

Step 4. Add a name to the list and a description

The name of the lists has a maximum of 25 characters. Choose a name that highlights what those profiles have in common. For example: Influencers, journalists, friends, etc.

5. There are two privacy options : the public one where users can see your list, who they are and even subscribe to it. In the private option only you can see the list, its content and nobody can subscribe.

Step 5. List privacy

6. Once the list is saved, start adding users to your list from the search engine or from the people you follow. ☺

Step 6. Search for users

To add people to the list

7. Continuing the previous steps, now look for the users you want to have in the list. For example, I look for influencers.

8. Found the profile, click on the 3 points .

Step 8. Click on options

9. In the drop-down menu choose the "Add or remove from a list" button .

Step 9. Add or remove list

10. A drop down will show with a list of the lists you have created. When you select the list, it is automatically added .

Step 10. Select list

11. Ready! You already have users on your list. When you enter the list, the user's activity will appear.

Step 11. Review the list tweets

Twitter Analytics

Twitter Analytics helps you measure, analyze and understand the growth in the number of followers, tweets and Twitter Cards. Each of the data analyzed by Twitter Analytics has its control panel and it is possible to download the information in spreadsheets for manipulation.

To access Twitter Analytics, you must click on the "profile and configuration" button of your account and click on "Analytics".

TWITTER ANALYTICS

Next I mention the data that each control panel handles according to what you want to analyze.

Twitter Analytics for followers

If you plan to measure the followers you have, Twitter Analytics helps you get relevant and specific information about them , such as their interests, location and demographic data.

The information is handled graphically with the following information:

Interests

Location by country and city

User sex

To access this information, in Analytics, click on the "Audiences" tab. Make sure that in the box below your profile information, select "His followers".

Twitter Analytics for followers

Analytics for tweet activity

Twitter's analytical tool works to measure the interaction and activity of your tweets , as well as general data.

In the control panel you first find general interaction data: mentions, profiles that have followed you, as well as those that stopped following you during the month.

After this information, you will find detailed information about your tweets such as the type of tweet that has the best response from the audience, the hours with the best reach and the number of clicks it has. The analysis is accompanied with basic information such as number of RTs, Favorites and the answers that were obtained.

Knowing the information of the activity will serve to know what content your audience likes best.

If you want to have all this information at your fingertips, go to Twitter Analytics and click on the "tweets" tab.

Analytics for Twitter Cards

It is the most important data to analyze in Twitter Analytics because it provides information to improve the content of the tweets that handle any of our links and get more traffic to the website.

To visualize and analyze the information, we can choose between seeing the number of clicks in the URL of the tweet or the number of Retweets. You can modify all this information in the control panel.

In the case of Twitter Analytics, it does not matter if the account has a long seniority, since the profile data is obtained from July 2013.

Twitter Ads

Twitter also has its ad service like other powerful social networks. You can search for recognition, interaction or clicks. To be clear, Twitter Ads only promotes and advertises on Twitter - not like Facebook Ads where you can promote on Instagram.

If you ever dare to use Twitter Ads, I show you the goals you can achieve.

Recognition and scope

Interaction in the tweets

Get followers

Promotion of a website

Apps Promotion

The goal they use most in Twitter Ads is recognition and reach. Maybe you handle topics of interest, your profile is very well optimized and the only thing missing is a push with ads for your account to take off. ☺

To access Twitter Ads, you just have to go to "profile and settings" and click on "Twitter Ads".

How to access Twitter Ads

Quick Promote

It is an extension of Twitter Ads where you can promote a tweet faster with a wider audience and in fewer steps.

This type of promotion is used specifically for content that needs to be promoted at the moment.

The situations where it is used are as follows.

Product promotions for a limited time

Tweets live from an event

Users with high interaction rate

Images taken at the moment

To enter is very simple, just go to "profile and settings" and you will find the Promote Mode option.

Twitter Ads and quick promote

Twitter Cards

Twitter Cards are tweets in the form of cards where it presents relevant information such as title, summary, user and image. Twitter Cards are free, you just have to be registered in Twitter Ads.

Example of a Card to promote web page

Many users don't know Twitter Cards, but they should. Here some advantages.

Improve brand image

Increased visibility

Better reach

Increased interaction

Highest response number

Higher CTR

Use of Twitter cards

These are the 4 uses that you can give to benefit the profile of your company or your personal brand.

Generation of potential customers. Similar to Facebook ads to generate leads, capture data from users interested in your product.

Websites. The card presents relevant and summarized information on the website, including the website link to generate traffic.

Basic applications. Promote applications for mobile devices.

Image application The same previous use, only that an image is added to identify the application.

Where to create my Twitter cards for companies

Before creating your cards on Twitter for businesses, you need to know the number of your Twitter Ads account. To know them, you only enter Twitter Ads - previously explained - and in the URL you will see a code. That code is your account number for Twitter ads for companies, save it.

Twitter Cards homepage

Tools to maximize the benefits of Twitter for companies

Companies that seek to grow, invest heavily in tools that help improve the strategy and positioning of their account. I share a small list of the most used tools for Twitter for companies according to the most important actions.

To manage and monitor

Tweetdeck In addition to managing your account and programming, you can monitor different aspects in the same window. The best thing is that it is free and easy to handle.

Hootsuite The most popular tool for managing social networks. Unlike Tweetdeck, in Hootsuite you can monitor and manage many accounts at the same time. The good news is that there is a free version to start. ?

Buffer. Another of the most popular is a tool that helps you strategically program your content and shows you what your content has been with the greatest reach.

Audiense One of the most complete tools, where you can monitor your community, you can manage your followers, you can even know the best time to tweet and on what days .

For analytics

Tweetbinder This tool allows you to see complete

information about your shared links, tracking the hashtags you are using and everything you need to know about your Twitter account.

Bit.ly. The statistics it can offer you about your tweets is all you need. Bitly goes beyond a simple URL shortener hehe.

Metricool It offers you information about the reach, interaction and growth of your audience. The way in which Metricool shows its analytics, allows you to compare that growth with previous periods.

To interactuate

Retweet Rank. More than interaction, this tool offers you a report of the interactions your tweets have had, and also influence on your audience.

Mentionmapp This tool is super useful to know with whom of your followers it is worth interacting more, that is, it shows you which accounts you have had the most interaction with.

To search Trending Topics

Tweepsmap Based on location, Tweepsmap allows you to see where your audience is concentrated and shows the best times to tweet, as well as trends. It is based on numbers and percentages.

Trendmap With the help of an interactive map, this tool teaches you the trends and hashtags that are being used all over the world - I repeat, everything.

My initial recommendation is Audiense. It is a tool that helps you monitor and analyze your audience, interact more easily with your followers and automate direct messages when someone starts following you.

HOW TO EARN MONEY USING TWITTER

Twitter has long proven to be an effective tool for marketing businesses. Marketing specialists are discovering that the platform can be used to generate revenue directly. If you are not sure how to make money with Twitter, these are some of the ideas that will help you.

Its founders or first investors are not the only ones who have made a profit with this social network. Countless people and companies have harnessed the power of social networks to create new income opportunities.

If you want to know how to make money with Twitter these are some unique ways to make money with Twitter through some examples and some of the best practices to carry out.

HOW TO MONETIZE IN MEDIA STUDIO

How to activate monetization in Media Studio

For more information about our video ad solutions, contact your Twitter account manager.

Click on the Monetization button located in the top navigation bar.

Click Account Information in the drop-down menu that appears.

Complete all required fields on all three tabs:

Direction

Payment method

Tax Forms

Click on the Ready tab to complete the configuration.

How to monetize videos

For more information about our video ad solutions, contact your Twitter account manager.

Click on a video from the Media Studio library.

Click on the Monetization tab .

Click the Monetize this video button .

Select the corresponding content categories in the Tag your content section (select up to 2 categories per video).

If you don't want certain advertising categories to appear in front of your video, you can select the number of relevant categories in the Exclude tags section

Tip

Reduce too much tags; This may restrict the ad that could relate to your video.

If you don't want certain advertisers to associate with your video, you can enter these usernames manually.

HOW TO SET DEFAULT MONETIZATION SETTINGS

For more information about our video ad solutions, contact your Twitter account manager.

Click on the Monetization button located in the top navigation bar.

Click Settings in the drop-down menu that appears.

Turn on the Monetize all new videos with In-Stream Video Ads option if you want all recently uploaded videos to be automatically monetized.

Select the corresponding content categories in the Tag your content section (select up to 2 categories per video).

If you don't want certain advertising categories to appear in front of your video, you can select the number of relevant categories in the Exclude tags section

Tip

Reduce tags; This may restrict the ad that could relate to your video.

If you don't want certain advertisers to associate with your video, you can enter these usernames manually.

Click on Save . All new multimedia content to be monetized will have this configuration associated.

How to view estimated earnings by video

For more information about our video ad solutions, contact your Twitter account manager.

Click on a video from the Media Studio library.

Click the More statistics button .

Select a date range with the filter located in the upper right corner (whose default setting is a 7-day display).

Scroll down to the Estimated Earnings section to see the amount earned during that particular date range.

How to view publisher payment information (total earnings)

For more information about our video ad solutions, contact your Twitter account manager.

Click on the Monetization button located in the top navigation bar.

Click on Earnings in the drop-down menu that appears.

All payment information should appear, and be available for export.

CONCLUSION

In the world where more than 70% of internet users are involved on social networks, who spend at least one hour a day on social networks on average, we must infer that social networks have become a kind of reality in which people communicate, engage and, naturally, trust.

We also need to be aware that more than 60 percent of those users access social networks via mobile devices, with strong indicators that this percentage will only increase in the years to come.

In such a world, we have to admit that social networks are also part of the business world as a new dimension of reality. More than 90 per cent of advertisers say that they are or will use social networks for companies, while more than 60 per cent claim to have gained new customers via social networks.

The studies released by business professionals and advertisers support the fact that companies will benefit greatly from using social networks, which is why it has become part of business culture to incorporate such. That's why social media marketing is no longer considered on probation but has become an important part of the business world instead.

www.ingramcontent.com/pod-product-compliance
Lightning Source LLC
Chambersburg PA
CBHW052350220526
45465CB00003BA/1047